Learning to disagree

Peace and Economic Development in Ireland

GW01186204

Edited by
Bernard Harbor, Peter
1996

Published in 1996 by:
UNISON, 1 Mabledon Place, London, WC1H 9AJ, and
IMPACT, The Public Sector Union, Nerney's Court, Dublin 1

Design and layout by Artworkers

Acknowledgements

IMPACT and UNISON are grateful to the European Union's Trade Union Information Division and the Combat Poverty Agency's Promoting Common Interests grants scheme for contributing to the funding of this project. Their assistance is greatly appreciated.

Pamela Dooley, Ann McGovern, Patricia McKeown and the staff of the Belfast UNISON office put enormous effort into organising the conference from which this book developed, and Roisin Nolan at IMPACT assisted in the production of the book. Senan Turnball of Area Development Management gave very helpful advice in the early stages of the project and, later, Eve Barker of Artworkers met a very tight production schedule for the book. Thank you all very much.

Most of all, IMPACT and UNISON would like to thank all the participants and speakers listed in the appendix who not only made the initial conference a success, but also made this book possible.

Irish border region

—— Border

—— District council boundary (NI)
County boundary (Rep. of I.)

N

DONEGAL

Derry
DERRY

Lifford • Strabane
STRABANE

• Omagh
OMAGH

Dungannon
DUNGANNON

BELFAST

Lurgan
Brownlow
Portadown

Armagh

DOWN

Downpatrick •

LEITRIM

• Enniskillen
FERMANAGH

Monaghan
Clones
MONAGHAN

ARMAGH

Newry
NEWRY & MOURNE

Carrick on
Shannon

• Cavan

CAVAN

Dundalk

LOUTH

DUBLIN •

Foreword
Empowerment Through Partnership
President Mary Robinson

In February 1996, I was invited to open a conference organised by IMPACT and UNISON, the two main public service unions in Ireland, on the subject of empowerment through partnership. This subject is of crucial importance to the island of Ireland and the relationships between Britain and Ireland, something we were particularly conscious of as the conference took place in the week following the Canary Wharf bombing. The terrible atrocity in London was an appalling set back. As our sympathy went out to the victims and their families, I sensed that people throughout the island were stunned and sickened, worried and anxious.

The theme of the conference, and of this book which is based on the conference proceedings, is partnership, empowerment and change in society. It builds on a very powerful statement about the need to decommission 'mind sets' in our society, and it looks at that idea in the context of change - changing minds and attitudes on this island, in relationships between Britain and Ireland, and in relationships and interactions between people themselves.

At the 1995 UNISON conference, a delegate from Northern Ireland, Anna McGonigle, had explained that the year before she had somehow felt overwhelmed by the possibility of peace. Now, she was overwhelmed by the prospect of peace ending. She spoke of her pride in her union because it had taken on the responsibility of being an agent of change in the peace process. I place a great value on language, and I thought her words were a powerful affirmation of her union.

In fact, the trade union movement has been an agent of change in many positive ways on the island of Ireland. I witnessed that myself, in Belfast, when I visited a centre for the unemployed and took part in a seminar organised by Counteract. Since its establishment in 1992, Counteract has been working quietly and consistently, and with determination, on action programmes to combat and reduce intimidation and sectarianism in the work place. It was doing this during times of great difficulty and has continued to try to change attitudes, to alter perceptions and to be that agent of change.

By choosing the title 'Empowerment through Partnership', IMPACT and UNISON again committed themselves to be agents of change in the way power is exercised. It seemed particularly appropriate that this had been done under the joint auspicious of the two main public service unions, because the way power is exercised is a fundamental issue in society - and changing it is not easy.

Those who use and wield power are accustomed to exercising it, and to doing so their way. Whether addressing or analysing issues, putting forward policies and programmes, or putting forward solutions, they are used to making the decisions. UNISON and IMPACT were saying that it is time to develop new open listening partnership structures where, instead of one side having the power (and using it for the benefit of the recipients of that power), there would be a genuine commitment to partnership in its exercise.

I believe this is absolutely at the heart of the capacity of our society to move forward; to change in a way which may not seem central to the peace process but which is so important to it. It is vital to create broader changes in our society which would help to build peace, reconciliation and greater understanding.

My office as President is not one of political power. It is an office which stays out of policy making, preparing budgets, or bringing forward proposals. That has enabled me to listen to those who have a significant contribution to make, but have not been able to make it to the extent they could if the structures of society were different. I am referring to local communities and groups; those who know the problem on the ground, whom I meet on a daily basis, and who's work I admire. A number of them were represented at the conference and their testament in this book shows the potential value of the partnership approach.

Local community groups throughout the island of Ireland have identified local needs, taken the initiative and harnessed energies in a very vibrant way, but have then come up against a blockage in the established power structure. In essence, it is a question of attitude.

If only those with power, and who wish to exercise it well, would listen and incorporate the experience of those who have first hand knowledge of the reality of the situation on the ground. The result would transform ideas of leadership and of decision-making.

That is the theme of this important and thought-provoking book. It is about sharing power through partnership. The potential to change our way of doing things carries far beyond the economic and social spheres. It is about building a greater respect for each other. A greater willingness to reach out to the other. A capacity to work in partnership and to reach accommodation.

I have a huge sense of wasted potential on this island. I see so much energy and commitment being harnessed with great determination at local level, and involving a significant percentage of women. I listen to their frustration at not having the capacity to influence policies. If we take the various ways in which this is evident on the ground, we can see that there is a real opportunity for improving gender balance in partnerships of power. This is another dimension of the greater potential to include those who are marginalised and who feel excluded.

This is relevant to the broader sense of what is happening throughout the island of Ireland at present. People have begun to reflect, to think and open up to each other. Important but subtle shifts are taking place. We are realising the importance of dialogue, of reaching out and understanding the other persons' point of view. That is true in the work place and in broader economic and social situations. It's also increasing true at the political level - a very important development which we must not allow to be dissipated.

We must rededicate ourselves to building on that willingness to open up to the other and carry it further. That is exactly what this book focuses on in the theme - empowering through partnership. It is about respecting, listening and evolving structures that allow the participation of people who are less confident of themselves in a public capacity.

Those who are influential in the public service unions, those in the civil service and in executive positions, have the capacity to build better links to bridge that partnership. It does require a mind set that is positively disposed to doing just that. If you stand back from it, it won't happen; you have to be engaged. You have to meet the group, the local community, the women's centre, the small marginalised rural group, or whatever it may be. You must meet them more than half way. You must make it easier for them to tell their story, easier for them to describe what they feel is important. You have to go the extra distance so you can meet in the middle and there can be a genuine partnership. Not 'them and us'. Not 'we decide for your benefit because we know what benefits you'. The person who really knows is the person who is directly affected.

We are fortunate in having external support to develop these possibilities. We have had great support from the United States and from the European Union (EU) in the context of the peace process. This was reflected in the Washington economic conference, the interest of the Clinton administration and President Clinton's visit to Northern Ireland and Dublin last year. We have had the EU initiative programme which is geared precisely to encourage this kind of partnership in power sharing to create local employment and provide opportunities for local communities.

This external support is vital because, behind all the uncertainty and fear there is an overriding worry that nothing will really change. I don't think that is the case. There are significant changes taking place already which can be pushed forward to make a genuine difference. Among those changes is how those with power use that power in the context of economic decisions and service provision; in the context of social decisions of inclusiveness, and ensuring that there is a sense of partnership. We must foster that climate of change - that sense at local level that their views are taken on board and that they are involved in how decisions are taken and implemented.

The authors of this book are the practitioners. They represent the public sector, business, trade unions and community groups who want to develop this type of partnership and interaction. That's why, when I was invited to open the conference, I emphasised the importance of the theme. I believe it is even more crucial now. We need a sense of moving forward. We need the capacity to move together in an empowering partnership from the bottom up and from the top down.

If all of us, on reading this book, accepted in our different ways the responsibility to be agents of change, we would be more than half way there.

Section One
Introduction

Partnership, Democracy and Economic Development

Bernard Harbor and Peter Morris

Bernard Harbor is the Information Officer for IMPACT, Ireland's leading public sector trade union. Peter Morris is National Research and Policy Director for UNISON, the leading public sector union in Northern Ireland and Britain's largest trade union.

This book covers large themes on the relatively small canvas of the island of Ireland. It deals with issues of democracy and power, peace and economic development, and the relationship between the governors and the governed. It describes innovative models of economic development that are potentially responsive to the needs of the long-term unemployed, not least because they involve people from the communities which are themselves hurt by poverty and deprivation. Because these are questions that trouble people across the globe, the partnership experiences described here may well inform debates about civic governance, unemployment and poverty in Europe, the United States and elsewhere.

The papers in this book are based on contributions to a path-breaking conference, organised by UNISON and IMPACT, which took place in Northern Ireland early in 1996. The conference brought together delegates from across borders and community divides, including representatives of various political traditions in Northern Ireland, the Republic of Ireland and Britain. The participants brought with them a wide variety of economic experiences and perspectives - from private industry, trade unions, local and central government, the European Union, the statutory sector and community and voluntary groups. All the participants were practitioners in economic development and partnership and this book focuses on practical policies for peace, jobs and economic development, based on their experiences and insights.

The conference took place in the week following the end of the IRA cease-fire and its detonation of a bomb in London's Canary Wharf. This inevitably dampened the optimism that had been palpable in Northern Ireland in the preceding 18 months. But it also underscored the urgency of finding new approaches to economic and social development that could sustain employment and contribute to peace and reconciliation in Ireland.

There was a practical reason for focusing on partnership as a central theme. When establishing the European Union (EU) fund for peace and reconciliation in Northern Ireland and the border counties, balanced community representation was one of the early conditions laid down by Regional Affairs Commissioner Monica Wulf Matthies. In order to access the funds, representatives from divided communities (including their political representatives) would be required to sit down together and reach agreement on how money should be invested, where it should be targeted, and who should gain from it. European investment was also made conditional on the establishment of 'partnership boards' made up of community representatives, trade unions, employers, statutory agencies and local political representatives.

Although this partnership model had been quite well established in the south, it was relatively new to Northern Ireland. There was, and still is, considerable scepticism and trepidation about how it could work and what its results would be. Our conference sought to bring together the very different perspectives on 'partnership' from Britain and Ireland, north and south.

The experiment emphasised one of the major themes of this book - that partnership is not an easy alternative to traditional models of economic development. Nor is it a substitute for conflict. Opposing interests are real and have to be faced up. What the partnership model does offer, however, is a mechanism for recognising and respecting differences and dealing with disagreement in a positive way. In this way, it holds out the possibility of accommodating differences while working together from the common ground that does exist to forge practical solutions to the problems of economic and social decay. In so doing, it can help establish the trust, and the economic and social breathing space, which are prerequisites for a sustainable peace.

Social partnership

The concept of social partnership is not new in European politics. It has been intrinsic in the post-war development of European economies. But it is relatively new in the Irish and United Kingdom context, particularly in the field of public administration. Bringing together trade unionists and community activists from Britain and Ireland involved bringing together three very different experiences of partnership in local economic development.

Those from Britain tended to associate partnership with government policies hostile to local democracy. To them, partnership was primarily to do with unrepresentative quangos and privatisation.

Practitioners from Northern Ireland shared some of these suspicions. They suspected that as funds came into their communities through partnerships, they would flow out of the statutory sector at least at the same rate. Some feared that partnerships would merely create another layer of bureaucracy, another hurdle for local community projects to jump. At worst, they feared the work of local community projects and activists would be sacrificed to private sector interests or political agendas. All of these reservations are voiced in papers in this book.

However, trade unionists and community activists from the south of Ireland brought a very different perspective based on the model of social partnership developed in Ireland since the late 1980s.

Since 1987, successive national agreements between Irish governments, employers organisations, trade unions and farmers' representatives have bought economic stability with high growth, low inflation, falling public debt and rising real wages. There is a consensus that these agreements - which involve wage restraint along with agreement on economic and social policies - have been an essential ingredient in Ireland's economic regeneration. Each of the partners has reservations about elements of the national agreements; employers want more flexibility on pay and industrial restructuring, trade unions are unhappy with the failure of national agreements to tackle low pay or make deep inroads into unemployment; both want substantial reform of the tax system. But very few advocate a return to the old way of doing business.

As it has developed, the Irish model has also attempted to include groups from the so-called 'third strand'. In particular, the influential National Economic and Social Forum (NESF) has formally brought those groups, including the unemployed, women, travellers, youth, disability groups and environmental groups, into the national social and economic debate. The principal economic actors (government, employers and trade unions) retain the strongest influence over the negotiation and operation of national agreements. For some, they remain advocates for the 'insiders' who have relatively secure work. Nevertheless, the national agreements do address the question of redistributing the gains of economic development, including to those out of work.

By the early 1990s, a partnership model for local, area-based economic and social development was officially adopted, specifically in response to the challenge of long-term unemployment. This approach emphasises partnership and dialogue between the social partners, the statutory sector and the voluntary and community sector. It stresses the importance of integrating economic and social actions to create a more comprehensive and integrated response to unemployment and social need. Crucially, it involves the active participation of local communities in the planning and implementation of local job creation and economic development initiatives. There have been tensions here, particularly in the relationship between partnerships and local elected representatives. But the model stands as a tried and tested approach to local economic development which has won converts from among the sceptical in politics, business, trade unions and the community sector.

The establishment of partnership as the foundation of Ireland's economic and social model – and the tangible evidence of its success at national and local level – can inform and give practical substance to recent debates about the 'stakeholder economy' which suggest that corporate responsibility goes beyond a responsibility to shareholders to include employees, customers, suppliers, communities and the wider economy.

Tackling unemployment: models for economic development
One contributor to this book evokes an image of a bridge between the world of unemployment and the world of work. The partnership programmes are about helping people to cross the bridge through practical and focused measures. Best practice involves setting concrete but achievable goals in this regard, such as Dublin Northside Partnership's target of creating 4,400 jobs between 1996 and 1999.

To be successful, partnerships must deliberately avoid becoming marginal in their activities and impact. The involvement and active participation of a wide range of relevant interests is essential. Partnerships are about dialogue; people with very different backgrounds, perspectives, interests, and styles of organising, sitting round the table together to achieve something in their common interest.

A number of contributors note how the dynamic of partnerships - and even the language of different partners - can change as people work together and develop relationships. Charged words like 'exploitation' or 'state bureaucracies' can be replaced with more constructive debates about problems and means of overcoming them. This requires a focus on practical issues. How can jobs be created or attracted to the area? What training or encouragement do local people need in order to become more employable? How can they be placed in specific workplaces, in jobs or work experience schemes? How can training be provided for particular groups of people? How should school and formal education be linked up to the programmes? And so on.

Once you focus on 'achievable goals' the question arises of how far local partnerships operate on the margins of economic development. No matter how successful a local partnership is, the fact remains that the decision of a large multi-national company can still devastate a local community. Your partnership might set a target of creating 300-400 jobs over three or four years, while the closure of a large local factory can mean the loss of two or three thousand jobs overnight. The conclusion must be that local programmes do not present an alternative to national and European-level measures to gain some control over the direction of multi-national investment and capital. Nor are they a substitute for the political process or community and trade union struggle. But their practical engagement with the long-term unemployed and disadvantaged communities should be a central element of local, national, and European economic and social policy-making. While local partnerships have obvious limitations in an increasingly international economy, they must be not be seen as peripheral to economic development.

Even if partnerships are limited in their ability to influence the decisions of large employers, they can help create jobs and put people back into the world of work. As such, theirs remains an important contribution. But evidence suggests that a good local partnership can reinforce the commitment of private investors and employers in a locality. Partnership is about engagement and participation, building the confidence of all partners in their community as well as the confidence of individuals in themselves and their power to shape their lives.

As well as being about economic democracy, the partnership process could represent an extension of the European model of social democracy that evolved in a period of high employment and effective social protection. That model recognised a strong role for trade unions, in partnership with employers, in the economic government of the country. Partnership extends a role to community organisations, in partnership with unions, employers and the statutory sector, in the economic and social regeneration of the locality.

New models of civic governance

In recent years there has been, if not a crisis, at least an erosion of confidence in the traditional forms of local government which emerged both in Britain and Ireland over the last hundred years. The decline in resources available to local government, the loss of control over revenue raising and accompanying centralisation of control, together with privatisation (especially, but not exclusively, in Britain and Northern Ireland) have reduced the ability of local government to provide services, still less to intervene in the local economy.

More fundamentally, politicians at local and national level have come to be seen by many as divorced from the people they represent.

There is a cynicism about public life and the political process. One spin-off of this is that many people who have been, or might have become, active in local politics now look to community groups, housing and tenants associations or single-issue campaign groups to provide a democratic expression and deliver social change.

Against this background, the partnership process can assist in the development of new models of governance by bringing together apparently irreconcilable forms of 'representative' and 'participative' democracy and reconciling some of the tensions between them.

Representation is the traditional form of local government democracy, and it is also familiar in trade unions. On the foundation of regular elections (which make it very broadly and formally, if not immediately, accountable) it involves the well-articulated delegation of authority from one level to the one above. Even under a system of proportional representation (as in the Republic of Ireland) it is a 'winner takes all' system which often fails effectively to work on the basis of consensus or deal with the democratic deficit which comes with abstention.

The tradition of participative democracy also has deep historical roots. Its defining characteristic is that it involves people in decision making. It allows individuals to have their say and the leadership that evolves is immediately accountable. But its has weaknesses too. Its impermanent structures and incomplete participation (you cannot compel people to participate and people can't always bear a constant involvement in the decision making process) questions the accountability of many participative organisations. Indeed, one of the most frequent criticisms of community and campaign groups is 'who do they represent?'

In fact, both traditions have strengths as well as weakness and both are valid. Formal partnerships bring them together, or at least force them to confront each other. It demands that both recognise the existence and validity of each other. In so doing, it can also help them to better understand their critics - to see themselves as others see them. This is what one contributor describes as being 'bilingual about power'.

New voices: democratic renewal and peace

The process of partnership has also brought new voices into the field of local economic and social development. One striking feature of the IMPACT-UNISON conference was that the voices of business, of women and of the community organisations were heard most effectively and most strikingly. In particular, there was a sense that women, whose presence had been largely hidden, were becoming leading actors in partnership and were bringing with them a new language and agenda.

One of the potential benefits of the partnership process is that a more inclusive form of democracy might develop; a rougher edged but more open democracy which learns from the difficult and painful experience of overcoming the sectarian divide. The participants in partnership must not become gatekeepers, preventing others from entering with their own (sometimes awkward or unsettling) concerns, priorities and questions. It is a matter of genuine openness - a responsiveness to the real concerns of the community as it develops - not simply appropriating a few more people or vocal groups into a prevailing clique.

These new forms of economic and social development are integral to the peace process itself. Inequality and social exclusion are the enemies of peace as surely as the gun and the bomb. One of the most hopeful signs at the UNISON-IMPACT conference was a palpable commitment to build a peace process through concrete economic action, despite the fears that the Canary Wharf bomb had unleashed. In her foreword to this book, President Mary Robinson talks about the need to 'decommission mind sets.' This applies not only in Northern Ireland but in Britain and across Europe. It applies to private industry, the public sector and trade unions as well as to government. The tentative efforts of brave individuals, organisations and enterprises, carried out in the harsh glare of the Northern Ireland peace process, may prove to have equal relevance to the wider renewal of the European model of social, economic and political development.

Section Two
Perspectives on partnership

Partnership and Public Services
Tony McCusker

Tony McCusker is Director of Making Belfast Work

Partnership has become the mantra of the moment. Partnerships are going forth and multiplying, keenly adopting mission statements and strategic visions. Does this represent a new form of governance where key agencies across all sectors stop playing solo and instead join a symphony of effort to tackle problems of decline and social need? Or is this simply a passing fad? The jury is still out. But it is useful to retrace approaches to public services over the last century to see where partnership fits into the pattern. For the sake of simplicity and clarity I intend to cover these under what I call the five 'Ps'.

The five Ps

The first 'P' dates back over a hundred years when cities and civic life were largely shaped by the patrician decrees of political grandees and corporate benefactors. Most people were meant to be the grateful recipients of the largesse bestowed by their social and moral superiors. Philanthropy was summoned to fill the gaps created by a weak and often penal public welfare system. Even the voluntary sector at that time largely assumed that mantle of charity based on 'care-taking' the poor rather than challenging poverty.

The positive monuments of this period - libraries, museums, public parks - bear witness to the dynamism of these patrician figures, keen to leave their imprint behind. But these aesthetics and amenities shared space with slums and open sewerage, the dwelling place of the huddled labouring masses. The patrician era of Victorian times certainly left its signature in the form of some grand buildings and spectacular infrastructure, but this progress was humbled by

19

the human misery and insecurity that beset most families in the period.

The second 'P' came with the paternalist public bureaucracies of the modern welfare state after 1945. On the plus side, the welfare state represented a serious and systematic attempt to address five key social problems. Want was to be tackled by a more comprehensive social security scheme based on social insurance; disease was to be treated by a National Health Service, free at the point of use and based on medical need; ignorance was to be erased by a free secondary education system offering equality of opportunity; squalor was to be replaced by decent housing within an overall strategic planning system; and idleness was to be banished by the delivery of full employment.

Importantly this new social contract made the first shaky attempt to relate government to people as citizens. The ideal of civil rights (to vote, join political parties and protest) was now tied to the idea of social rights (to decent housing, health care, education and the right to work). But the edifice remained shaky. The vast public bureaucracies spawned to deliver these services treated people as clients or patients, but rarely as citizens. It was still a question of handing down to people rather than giving people the ownership of these services. Public servants could too often appear to be the public's masters. This was evident, for example, when whole communities were bulldozed and scattered under the remit of slum clearance when the old tenements were replaced by the new tenements of ghastly tower blocks and bleak concrete enclaves.

By the 1960s, people wanted less of the paternalism which allowed experts to frame social habitats for others which they would never dream of sharing themselves. People wanted a say in their own lives, and this brought us to the third 'P' - public participation.

A series of official reports started to acknowledge that public services could only meet their mission if they involved the public more in their design and delivery. Among others, the Plowden Report recommended greater parental involvement in schools; the Seebolm Report suggested new ways for social services to accommodate feedback from their clients; and the Skeffington Report spoke of the need to facilitate public participation in urban planning.

But in the late 1970s other forces intruded before this trend took root. As the economy hit the rocks, doubts were raised as to whether welfarism has become a bloated empire that the country could no longer afford. More fundamentally, the claim was made that the welfare state had become the nanny state, one that cushioned people not only from risk but also from the repercussions of their own irresponsibility. It was said that a dependency culture had been created which sapped enterprise and eroded the work ethic with penal taxation.

In this context the move in the 1980s was to the fourth 'P' - privatisation. This involved an attempt to encourage individuals to secure more of their own welfare needs though private provision. Alongside this there was an elevation of the role of the voluntary sector and a search for areas of public provision where it could step in for the statutory sector. Government was to be less about direct provision and more about enabling. Far from being the solution, big government was seen to be part of the problem.

But, although there has been an increased take-up in areas like private health insurance and private pension schemes and an expansion of voluntary self-help initiatives most people continue to rely on public services. So there has been a second stage of privatisation. In search of economy and efficiency, certain characteristics of the private sector have been imported into the public realm. Thus we have seen attempts to install internal markets and to deploy market testing. The language of choice has been introduced. No longer seen as clients, but rather as consumers, the public has been encouraged to raise its expectations about quality. This new culture is exemplified in the concept of citizens' charters, which seek to set best practice standards and more transparency in the operation of public bodies.

Now, in the 1990s, the fifth 'P' - partnership - has entered the stage. It implies that equity must stand alongside economy and efficiency as a measure of effective performance. It implies that good governance will not come from a return to old-style distant public bureaucracies. It implies that no one sector has all the resources or all the answers. It implies that decision-making must be closer to those most affected by decisions. It implies that people will better appreciate services if they have more ownership of their development. It implies that drawing people together from diverse experiences and viewpoints offers the best chance of creating new thinking for the new times. And it also implies that what can be achieved by sectors acting co-operatively is greater than the sum of what each can achieve separately.

Back in the 1960s we talked of participation, now we speak of partnership. Then, deprivation was deemed to be 'multiple', now it is 'multi-dimensional'. Then, we talked of the poor, today we refer to the socially excluded. Then, we heard of the need for community self-help, now we speak of community empowerment. Then, we were told of the importance of policy co-ordination, now we applaud the virtue of integrated planning. A cynic might charge that because we could not change the problem, we simply changed the vocabulary. But partnership is potentially more than a semantic revisit of old concepts.

No panacea

But problems remain. The new partnerships are being nurtured in a cold climate of quick remedies for deep social malaise. For instance, in the years ahead the public purse is likely to be squeezed tighter and agentisation will see a significant rearrangement of the public sector. Some say that the drive to a more competitive economy in Europe risks shoving many at the bottom of the social scale to the furthest fringes of the labour market. Moreover, it's hard to set up new partnerships without having some relevant agencies in serious disagreement, and refusing to partake. Such rancour leaves many fledgling partnerships trying to build a firm foundation from the bricks that their critics throw.

Yet, in spite of the many critics in all sectors, capable of wrecking the process, there are many more who see the advantages. Many of the partnerships addressing regeneration within Northern Ireland will work at the cutting edge of the tension between strengthening a competitive economy and targeting social need. We can't avoid this challenge if we want to avoid whole cities and regions being divided between those in work and those on welfare. By bringing these tensions around a negotiating and planning table, perhaps partner-

22

ships now offer the best chance of devising strategic ways forward.

There remain other practical reasons why partnerships need to be tried and tested, not least the fact that we have exhausted many other approaches. The partnership model is now central to public policy within the EU, with European funds increasingly tied to partnership structures. Similarly, trusts are looking increasingly for matching funding and assembling such funding packages entails collaborative relationships among different agencies.

Finally, there is a sixth 'P' which is definitely not on offer - that is panacea. There simply is none. But the culture of partnership offers some scope between hankering after the ways of old and fantasising about future utopias. As they say, 'between yesterday's regret and tomorrow's dream is today's opportunity'.

Building the Complex Circuitry of Partnership

Sir George Quigley KBC

Sir George Quigley is Chair of Ulster Bank Ltd. In 1994 he was appointed Chair of Co-operation North and the Northern Ireland Economic Council. He is also a member of the Executive Committee of the Economic and Social Research Institute in Dublin. Between 1990 and 1994 he chaired the Institute of Directors (Northern Ireland Division) and he was a member of the Fair Employment Commission from 1989 to 1993.

My theme is the interconnectedness of so many of the factors and circumstances that go to make up our world, and which presents opportunities for exploiting the synergy which results from sharing information, analysis and experience and from concerting action.

The model for today's successful company is one where everyone is linked in a chain of effort to achieve customer satisfaction. What is important is not simply how parts of a business work in isolation but how well they work together to meet corporate objectives. Traditionally, companies have been organised on functional lines into bureaucratic compartments focused on discrete tasks. The structure has consisted of vertical silos, each built on a narrow piece of what should be a seamless process. It is now recognised that managing these 'stove pipe' functions can obscure the line of vision to customers and that it will often be more appropriate to organise work in terms of processes. There is therefore much talk these days of the 'horizontal' company, with teams which transcend the old functional boundaries. In this model there is no room for functional foxholes.

Such companies major on continuous improvement and they recognise the crucial importance of employee motivation. So there is also much talk these days of the 'mutual gains enterprise', as an expression of company solidarity. Human resource considerations need to be factored in from the beginning, not added as an afterthought at the end. Appropriately adapted, there are obvious implications in this for the work of the public sector as well.

The experience of the successful economies teaches us that the 'enterprise capsule' is not just the individual firm. It is a cluster of interacting influences and interests. It is a network of companies in similar areas of business, along with their suppliers, the educational and research establishments and business support services of all kinds (including the financial services). This network forms a 'development block'. Real success in developing a location and in giving individual companies the best chance to succeed depends on getting the right cluster of investments. How we organise economic space is the 'X factor' which creates fertile ground for further related investments.

Shared vision

Since economic policy involves balancing equity and efficiency, all corners of the land want a place in the sun, a share of the action. In part, it is concerns around this issue which have promoted localities and voluntary and community organisations all over the island to take greater responsibility for their own welfare. As a consequence, it is no longer enough to talk about government and the market as the two key economic players. There is now a space between them occupied by a third player - that is, by a host of intermediate bodies such as local authorities and voluntary and community groups.

The challenge is how to obtain maximum synergy from the proper integration of the combined effort of government, private sector and these intermediate bodies, which comes from a shared vision. That was a key message from a seminar organised by the Northern Ireland Economic Council early in 1995, and a great deal more work needs to be done to make the partnership a reality.

There is increasing recognition that the pursuit of low inflation, which has been the dominant economic orthodoxy of the past decade, can be undermined if growth is sluggish and unemployment rises and remains stubbornly high. Multiple objectives - a cluster of objectives - need to be targeted. That is at the heart of a good deal of the present argument about movement to a single currency. The original European vision set great store by 'social solidarity' and the regional and social funds were shaped on that principle. The challenge to achieve it still remains. Without it, economic growth is

25

impaired. But how that solidarity is achieved will also define the limitations on growth in a ruthlessly competitive world.

Tony Blair's 'stakeholder' speech has restored to the agenda the issue of how one achieves at macro level the alignment of all the interests relevant to a prosperous society. At micro level, the private sector wrestles with the same issue. In that case the variables are customers, suppliers, employees and owners, in the form of shareholders.

For nearly ten years now in the south, there has been a process of consensual economic management involving government and the social partners which, however it may be open to criticism in detail, has produced remarkable growth. If you have a rapidly growing economy, you can at least do something with it, just as it is easier to change direction in a car which is moving than in one whose wheels are spinning and sinking deeper in the sand. There are aspects of this experience in partnership which could well be replicated in the north.

Long-term unemployment

Take an issue like long-term unemployment, which is the key social and economic problem to be addressed if disadvantage is to be seriously tackled both north and south. So far as the north is concerned, the demand for jobs will materialise if peace can be restored and, equally important, provided we get political stability and certainty. I would be more worried about the supply side of the equation. Short-term unemployment is now down almost to the UK level. Our problem is how to turn the long-term unemployed into a usable labour reserve which can be effectively mobilised for the conventional labour market. If we cannot crack the problem, economic growth can be severely curtailed and social stability jeopardised. The long-term unemployed are 'outsiders' denied the most obvious form of participation in society - a job.

Resolving the problem will call for changes in the education system; in how we deal with school leavers who cannot find jobs; in the whole system of social welfare; in training; and in the attitude of business. It is a 'systems' problem which will not yield to isolated, discrete initiatives. The 'stove-pipe' approach, to use my earlier figure of speech, will not work. Nor will incremental change which merely nibbles at the edges of the issue. In education, a systems approach is required. A sound education policy designed to provide genuine equality of opportunity has to be set in the context of a comprehensive policy for dealing with disadvantage.

Health

A welcome feature of the draft DHSS consultative paper is that it purports to be a strategy for health and not just for the health service. In other words, it recognises that the promotion of a positive sense of well-being and the prevention of illness depends on a host of factors including lifestyle, good housing, job security and adequate income. All these factors, complemented by an effective health service, must coalesce to produce the kind of outcome which we should really be measuring.

However, the DHSS paper is unfortunately weak on how the principle of partnership can be applied within the health service to include all the links in the chain which add value, including primary and community care, hospital services and so on. If the functional split between those who purchase care and those who provide it is to work sensibly, we must develop a partnership model - partnership between the management executive and the rest of the system; between purchasers and providers; and, very importantly, between providers themselves, whether they be in the same sector or in different sectors.

Partnership sourcing is increasingly the name of the game in the private sector. Within banking, developing durable relationships is the order of the day. Within an adequate resource framework for the health service, five year contracts, with in-built price and quality criteria and performance milestones, would solve many of the current problems. Such a system would also encourage providers not just to benchmark each other but also to share experience and exchange best practice freely, thereby jacking up standards all round.

The arts

The Northern Ireland Economic Council has recently published a study which shows the need not only to cultivate the contribution which the arts make to quality of life but also to exploit to the full their contribution to the economy. Cultural tourism is now recognised as a necessary component of any strategy for tourism. Business and the arts are interacting productively. Because arts administrators too face management challenges, COTHU, the business council for the arts in the south, operates a programme called INFORM in partnership with 24 of COTHU's corporate members, including Ulster Bank. These members provide places for arts managers on training courses alongside their contemporaries from business. Some of them organise a number of 'arts only' courses.

Openness and honesty

Partnership is now happening world-wide as regions and companies network and form strategic alliances of all kinds. Borders remain but they have become porous. The barriers are down. I am delighted and proud to have been - and to be - actively involved with many others in promoting the potential of the whole island as a natural economic zone. If the partnership principle is driving forward movement all over the world, why not in Ireland? World-wide, competition between countries and regions remains intense. What is new is the recognition that it does not preclude active co-operation as well.

Co-operation and partnership, in a whole host of areas - and I have been only illustrative - will take many forms. It will vary according to the issue to be addressed and the skills and experience which each partner brings. The institutional form which the partnership takes will also depend on the context. Some partnerships will be loose (but none the less useful for that) whilst others will be tight, with responsibilities carefully specified.

Openness and honesty and a willingness to face contentious issues will be key. Joint ventures, even between partners in the private sector, have to be worked at. Team building is never easy, but we should not always opt for ready-made compatibility. Research findings tell us that diverse teams are slower to get up steam, but when they do they are more effective.

Trust is an essential ingredient. The gurus are telling us that non-economic as well as economic factors contribute to economic success. It has been put this way: Excessive individualism and the prosecution of self-interest is, paradoxically, an economic dead-end. Distrust operates as a tax on all forms of economic activity. This trust is embedded in the country's social institutions and culture. It constitutes its social capital. Countries which possess it have the ability to undertake collective endeavours without detriment to the pursuit and achievement of individual benefit. Isn't that what partnership is all about? Partnership can generate trust. Trust in turn fosters partnership. Both are essential to create a climate conducive to peace and to translate that peace into opportunity. We therefore need to be open to the opportunities for partnership. Partnerships, networks, clusters - there is no other way.

To reinforce the point as graphically as I can, may I wax a little lyrical in conclusion and refer to some favourite lines from the American poet Walt Whitman, whom you could think of as the great poet of social inclusion. He describes the noiseless, patient spider launching forth 'filament, filament, filament out of itself, ever unreeling them till the gossamer thread catch somewhere.' The responsibility we all bear on this island to do just that - to build the complex circuitry which gives life and dynamism to the peace process - is now greater than ever.

Investing in Peace

Peter Cassells

Peter Cassells is General Secretary of the Irish Congress of Trade Unions (ICTU).

The Irish Congress of Trade Unions (ICTU) has 450,000 members in the Republic of Ireland and 220,000 in Northern Ireland, making it probably the largest organisation in the north. There are people of all political opinions and none, and people of all religious affiliations and none, among ICTU's northern membership. This has enabled people to debate and discuss economic and social issues without the tensions and difficulties which normally operate within the community. It is a great credit to people in Northern Ireland, that they have been able to hold the Irish Congress of Trade Unions and the trade union movement together.

Investing in Peace, ICTU's interim programme for social and economic reconstruction in Northern Ireland, was published immediately after the announcement of the cease-fire. ICTU took the view that ending violence was a crucial part, but only a part, of the process of creating a new peaceful and stabilised society in Northern Ireland; a society in which economic prosperity, full employment and equality of opportunity could become the norm. Therefore, our strategy argued very strongly that the cease-fire, though essential, had to be accompanied by an economic and social programme for reconstruction.

The programme deals with three areas. The first is economic issues, including a special programme to tackle long-term unemployment, tax incentives, research and development, tourism and developing co-operation and trade across the border. The second area is community and social issues including housing, community development, social services, health and child care. The third is the area of justice covering inequality, policing, victim support, the rehabilitation of prisoners, changes in the administration of justice and a bill of rights.

ICTU regards all of these as being very closely inter-linked and, whilst they are set out in separate chapters in our programme, we believe it vital that they are addressed together in an integrated way and in parallel with the peace process. It would make a big difference to people on the ground if they could see an integrated reconstruction programme alongside the peace process.

Economic reconstruction

The problem of long-term unemployment is key to our economic approach for the redevelopment of the Northern Ireland economy. We argue very strongly in the document that money formerly spent on security must be left in Northern Ireland to tackle long-term unemployment and create real jobs in local communities.

We also put forward priorities for investment under the European Union (EU) programme for peace and reconciliation, which covers Northern Ireland and the border counties of the south. We don't just want it to be spent on dual carriageways, highways and other infrastructure developments so that people say we have the best roads and infrastructure in Europe but we still have communities with very high levels of unemployment, enormous levels of deprivation, and very little interaction and reconciliation.

We therefore called for two specific criteria to be applied to projects supported by EU funds. The first was to target areas of greatest social need. These might be geographical areas of need in Belfast, Derry, Strabane, or the border regions. It also meant prioritising the needs of the long-term unemployed and community development. That was very difficult to argue for because on the other side people believed that if the money was earmarked for community groups, it would be squandered in search of local groups which have no idea about real business development and job creation. They argued that the only way to make progress was to move in a few factories and high profile projects.

The second criteria we put forward was that there should be a partnership approach with the full involvement of all communities. In the Republic we have had tripartite involvement (of government, employers and trade unions) in a wide range of key areas including employment, equality, health and safety and economic and social policy generally. But in Northern Ireland the government was unwilling to concede partnership because it would effectively undermine government policy on trade unions and other areas. They argued that very strongly with us, but ICTU very strongly said that, in the Republic, the partnership model had proved to be the only effective way to tackle long-term unemployment in local areas.

The European Commission, and particularly Monica Wulf-Matthies, the Commissioner with responsibility for the peace and reconciliation programme, insisted that the two principles of targeting areas of greatest social need and local community involvement were in the programme.

New ways of working

Difficult as it proved, arguing for the inclusion of these funding criteria is the easy part. On the ground people are expecting quick results in terms of jobs, new facilities and new ways of working. On the other hand public servants and administrators will get frustrated. To them, local community groups can be frustrating to work with because they are not highly structured organisations like ourselves (who are probably over structured in terms of our rules and regulations).

Whatever the challenges of this approach, it must be accepted that relying on existing mechanisms for delivery of a reconstruction programme is fraught with difficulties. Existing mechanisms will not directly engage disadvantaged groups or the local communities which have suffered the most from violence. Existing structures will tend to reinforce the status quo and will, therefore, fail to impact on people in areas of greatest disadvantage who most need to see tangible benefits if the peace process is to be meaningful to them.

Tackling Poverty and Inequality - A Perspective from the South

Sarah Craig

Sarah Craig is a Research Officer at the Combat Poverty Agency in Dublin. She is the author of Progress Through Partnership, (Combat Poverty Agency, 1994), the report of the final evaluation on the Programme for Economic and Social Progress (PESP) pilot initiative on long-term unemployment.

Between 1991 and 1993 a pilot programme was run in 12 areas of the Republic of Ireland to test out an area-based response to long-term unemployment. The pilot has since become the model for area-based economic and social development in the south.

In many respects it was a radical initiative, emphasising partnership and dialogue between the social partners, the statutory sector and the voluntary and community sector. It stressed the importance of integrating economic and social actions to create a more comprehensive and integrated response to unemployment and social need. It involved the active participation of local communities in the planning and implementation of the initiative. In many ways, it challenged the centralised and compartmentalised Irish administrative system to develop a more flexible, integrated and decentralised approach.

Voluntary and community sector involvement
The experience showed that partnership relationships designed to combat inequality, poverty and social exclusion work best with the participation of, and consultation with, the community and voluntary sector (as well as the statutory sector and the traditional social partners). In the south, various initiatives have begun to recognise the community and voluntary sector as a formal and equal partner. That recognition raises issues about resources, as the voluntary sector has traditionally been insufficiently resourced for participation in initiatives of this kind.

It also highlights the need for training and induction for participation which does, of course, apply equally to the other more traditional sectors. It also highlights the need for a community development focus to ensure that those most marginalised and socially excluded are included in the process. The partnership approach also raises issues about community representation and accountability: How do you define community? How do you agree representation from the community and voluntary sector? How is the community and voluntary sector accountable to the wider community? These are all issues which we are still working through.

Partnership models and their effectiveness

Although the pilot partnerships were set up with the same broad structures and objectives, different approaches emerged at local level. Three working models can be identified:

The delivery approach where partnerships act as delivery agencies, identifying a need in the local area and taking on the responsibility for providing that service. This usually happened on a pilot basis where the locality lacked services.

The agency approach, similar to the first, but where partnerships move service delivery away from their own direct control towards independent or existing service providers. Therefore, the partnership takes a reduced role in delivery.

The brokerage approach where partnerships do not deliver specific services themselves, but act as support and policy structures. Their function is needs assessment and lobbying existing delivery agencies for changes in provision.

In many respects, the brokerage approach proved to be the most effective model because it strengthened and enhanced existing provision rather than undermining it. Rather than concentrating on additional resources, it looked at how resources were currently being managed and gave partnerships a role in innovative service provision and in testing different ways of working. In turn, this can influence agency policy at local, regional and central levels.

Influencing policy-making

Experience also shows a need for local partnership initiatives to influence the regional and national policy-making process. Generally, the experience of partnerships on the ground has been that it is easy to see where the problems are, but quite difficult to initiate change through the policy making process. One of the difficulties in the south is the compartmentalisation of public administration, where education, training and employment are the responsibility of separate government departments with quite different approaches. There is a need for an integrated and co-ordinated policy response across departments, directed at the issues of poverty, inequality and long-term unemployment.

Lessons from the partnership experience have influenced the implementation of the Local Development Programme (1994-1999) in which the emphasis is more on regeneration of communities of disadvantage. It has also influenced the design and implementation of the Irish Government's National Anti-Poverty Strategy (NAPS). The aim of NAPS is to ensure that poverty and social exclusion is built into the objectives of every department of government and every public agency. With these initiatives in place there is some optimism about how poverty and disadvantage can be tackled successfully.

Temple Bar in Dublin has benefitted from regeneration

HOMER SYKES/NETWORK

35

Tackling Poverty and inequality -
A Perspective from the North

Maggie Bierne

Maggie Bierne is the Research and Policy Officer of the Committee on the Administration of Justice in Belfast.

There is sometimes a misapprehension that human rights only cover civil and political rights. But the UN Universal Declaration of Human Rights covers the whole spectrum of rights and the Committee on the Administration of Justice is very much concerned about economic justice. In our work, we are trying to make human rights a reality for people by bringing international principles to bear on local realities, drawing from those principles and building our work within them. This paper tries to do the same in the context of partnerships and particularly the area of targeting social need.

The EU special programme for peace and reconciliation has very lofty principles which aim to benefit all communities in an equitable and balanced way, focusing on those areas and sections of the population suffering the most acute deprivation. It talks of having an immediate and visible impact and of helping those affected by the conflict to live together in mutual respect. The programme uses words like 'social inclusion'. It talks of the need for a flexible combination of economic and social measures to tackle the root causes of deprivation in Northern Ireland. Its priorities include jobs for the long-term unemployed, greater participation by women in the work force and improvements to the social and physical environment of areas deeply damaged by conflict and violence. It mentions particular measures to deal with the special difficulties of vulnerable groups like victims, children and prisoners. Its final principle says that the programme, and the management of the programme, should facilitate genuine bottom-up involvement by empowering local agencies and groups to participate in the direction and control of the spending.

These are very exciting ideas and concepts but it is very important that we make a reality of them. Often the language can remain beautiful in the documents, but actually making something of it on the ground is quite different. In particular, we need to explore structures by which these principles can be made a reality on the ground (other contributors in this section of this book contribute helpfully to our understanding of that challenge). We need, for example, to ensure that partnerships are representative and accountable. They must act with integrity and be inclusive. The partnerships we are now creating must meet those principles, both in their composition and in their ways of working.

As to the work to be undertaken by partnerships, one of the principles set down in the guidelines for the EU programme in Northern Ireland is that partnerships should work within the context of two government policies - TSN (Targeting Social Need) and PAFT (Policy Appraisal and Fair Treatment guidelines).

Targeting social need (TSN)

The objective of TSN is to tackle deprivation in areas of greatest social and economic need prioritising those areas, communities and economic sectors which have suffered most. Accordingly, partnerships have, as a priority, to identify the areas of greatest need and ensure that the projects which come to them meet TSN criteria. That means benefiting the most vulnerable and empowering people locally. It means attacking the underlying causes of disadvantage and meeting the EU criteria of inclusiveness.

Policy appraisal and fair treatment guidelines (PAFT)

Detailed PAFT guidelines were introduced by the Government in 1993 to ensure that issues of equality and equity condition policy-making in all spheres and all levels of government activity. They are meant to ensure that programmes, service delivery and policies take the various needs of our community into account and ensure that there is no discrimination, whether on the grounds of religious belief, gender, political opinion, marital status, ethnic origin, disability, age or sexual orientation.

As the guidelines were introduced some time ago, the fact that they are still very little known to the public and the lack of accounting for how they are applied, are serious criticisms. Another very serious problem is that they are merely guidelines, with no legal force. To be really effective, they must be put on a statutory basis. But the most important thing is that partnerships bring these guidelines into their operational activity to ensure that the work they do can really benefit the most vulnerable within our society and undermine the legacy of discrimination which many groups experience in our society.

I would like to give two examples of how these principles can be given practical effect. Recently, UNISON sought a judicial review against the Down and Lisburn Council, arguing they had not used the PAFT guidelines in their decision-making. In his judgement, Mr Justice Kerr rejected the view that PAFT guidelines were merely a "lofty aspiration". He said the Government, in introducing the policy, must have intended that the guidelines actually be used and be given some practical fulfilment. I hope the partnerships will be able to do this.

PAFT was also used recently to question the very serious cuts that were made in our ACE programmes when people questioned the implications of an across-the-board 25 per cent cut which might impact disproportionately on the most vulnerable groups in society. PAFT provides a mechanism by which local community groups can start challenging government policy and, in the case of the partnerships, can actually apply it to the projects coming forward. Partnerships should assess their projects, indeed their overall programme, against these criteria.

Both TSN and PAFT provide extremely important mechanisms for undermining the very serious inequalities in our society. My organisation has criticised the Government for failing to give genuine commitment to these programmes and really exploit their potential. I hope that the partnerships will prove to be a mechanism to give practical expression to the policies, and to ask challenging questions. Perhaps the partnerships will provide a role model for how government itself should be answering some of these questions.

A Blueprint for Good Enough Partnership Practice

Dr Mo O'Toole

Mo O'Toole is a lecturer in British Government and Public Policy at the University of Newcastle-Upon-Tyne. She has worked and published extensively on the design, operation and evaluation of partnerships and undertook an extensive study of the partnership in Castlemilk, a depressed estate on the outskirts of Glasgow.

It is reasonable to ask what is different about partnerships because many approaches to community self development, urban regeneration and good governance have failed. It has been proved time and again, in both the public and private sectors, that the involvement of people at the grass roots profoundly affects the success or failure of policy implementation. And evidence from partnership experiments shows that, when people have some control over the projects in their area, the projects have a longer life and are likely to bring better results.

Even in partnerships, communities' control is limited - but at least they have a handle on what is going on. That can bring the ability to participate in decision-making. With some control over local economic development and training, it can bring some control over employability as well as over labour power. It can bring people who have previously been excluded from decision-making into the process of defining services. It can help construct or enhance community identity.

It can also bring dialogue. So many cities are divided into different parts, with affluence divided from deep structural poverty. People in the satellite estates of our major cities may never see the centre as it is too expensive to visit and, with no money, there's no reason to go there. Those who live outside the areas where the social base has collapsed have no reason to visit them, so they never see what is going on in their own cities. So many people are cut off from the changes going on around them and feel powerless to influence the change. But engaging in dialogue through partnership offers that power back. Partnership can provide the reason for crossing the border. The bank manager involved in an inner-city partnership gains and understanding of - and a commitment to - an area she or he would never have considered before.

Today's partnerships embody those characteristics and they have the legitimacy of an instrument of government, if not the concomitant power. They are part of a new configuration of agencies which play a part in the way our cities are governed, alongside the traditional governmental structures. If we combine the characteristics of community self development, urban regeneration and modern governance, we are developing new ways of governing our cities and new values to inform more democratic types of economic regeneration. Because of this, any attempt to graft on the old ways of doing things is doomed to failure. If we do that with partnerships, they simply won't work.

Experience shows that some basic rules have to be followed if partnerships are to be both democratic and effective - there is a blueprint for good enough partnership practice! First, your community must know that the partnership is coming, what it represents, and what it does and does not aim to do. The views and input of the community should be sought out - they should be asked what the problems are and how to go about solving them.

Then the partnership board and team has to work out its objectives in tune with both 'top down' and 'bottom up' intentions. All agencies, including groups at the grass roots, need to be integrated with the partnership at this early stage. Each partner needs to spell out what they are there to do and what skills, talents and resources they bring. In effect, specific job descriptions need to be drawn up so that everyone is aware of their own and each other's obligations. It is important to be specific - what exactly can a private entrepreneur or community representative do for and with the partnership? If it is a short-life agency, this should also include planning for your exit from the area. One way of doing this is to lock everyone up in a hotel for the weekend and refuse to let them out until aims, objectives, responsibilities and a strategy are worked out.

Following that, there needs to be a formal consultation process where people can submit objections and alternatives before final agreement is reached by the partnership board. Throughout this process, an independent 'referee' and/or community advocate can be useful.

By this stage, everybody should be in a position to sign up to a 'code of conduct' or 'principles of operation'. This should be a mutual protection plan as well as a means to help implement the strategy. Without it, there can be immense temptation to act outside the agreed partnership objectives when under pressure from constituent organisations. Councillors will be under pressure to get particular projects funded. Private sector representatives have business to do here and deals to strike there. Community representatives will be told by their groups that they are on the wrong track and should try to change decisions at the next meeting. A 'code of conduct' helps the partners to keep to agreed objectives and policies.

The partnership must also make sure that monitoring systems are in place from the outset. Evaluation criteria and data sets should be agreed and retained. Monitoring allows the partnership to record achievements and change course or improve performance if achievements are not materialising. It also allows the collection of evidence of initiatives that can work or of recalcitrant poverty or unemployment.

The partnership should also draw up a map of every agency in the area, their capabilities and the work they are doing. Where possible, plans for development and improvement should be congruent, fitting together to minimise the waste of resources. You want to achieve the maximum possible impact when spending money and resources, so it is important to have an overall picture of allocations in the area.

The partnership should set out specific, realisable objectives. There is no point in aiming for hundreds of training places or thousands of square feet of commercial space. Don't aim for the biggest superstore in Europe or expect 5,000 jobs to be established in the lifetime of the partnership. Small things can make a difference and if you do get a big opportunity, it's a bonus. The partnership should have objectives that can be reached, and even these should not be set in stone. If there is a big problem with the objectives or they are not being achieved, change them. If you don't, all the partners will think they have failed.

After the initial period, meetings should be minimised. At first there will be board meetings, sub-committees, inter-agency meetings and community meetings. If these are not rationalised as the partnership matures, people will either stop coming or become confused or burnt out with meetings-fatigue. Too many meetings are as bad as too few. Having said that, it is important to network with other partnerships - particularly for community representatives. This can be done through inter-partnership meetings, conferences or twinning programmes.

Finally, when policy decisions are taken - such as new initiatives or changing tack - information from the work of the partnership and its impact should be evaluated and fed into the policy-making structures.

All partnerships are unique and they have a multitude of different structures and ways of working. But adherence to these principles of working can help most partnerships to succeed. Partnership is not the easiest way of managing local places and people but it is potentially the most rewarding. It can ensure that the places belong to the people who live in, work in and use them and that the people themselves become empowered, rather than divorced from and alienated by, society. Partnership is a process of learning and changing; of involving people in the decision-making processes that govern their lives. If we seize it as our own, we have some chance of shaping the decision-making of the future. Just as the trade union, the local council or local action group is a source of empowerment, so the partnership can become one too.

Section Three
Partnership, social inclusion and economic development

A Responsibility Shared: Partnership in the Republic of Ireland

Dermot McCarthy

Dermot McCarthy is an Assistant Secretary in the Taoiseach's Department in Dublin with responsibility for economic and social policy and European affairs.

In the Irish Republic, there has been a structured process of dialogue and agreement between government and the social partners at national level since 1987. This approach stemmed from the realities faced by a small open economy which learned the hard way that there are limits to the range of action which governments can employ to stimulate economic development and employment. We also learned, perhaps painfully, the interaction between public spending and taxation, and the impact which both have on disposable incomes. From the experience of the 1970s and 1980s, government and the key economic agents of society have developed a broadly shared analysis of the nature of Irish society and the Irish economy. From that shared analysis institutional supports for partnership have been developed at national and local level.

Partnership at national level

Three successive national programmes were agreed between government and the social partners between 1987 and the present day; the Programme for National Recovery (PNR), the Programme for Economic and Social Progress (PESP) and the Programme for Competitiveness and Work (PCW) which concludes at the end of 1996. As their titles suggest, the three programmes were born of slightly different contexts, but they shared a strategic emphasis on the need for economic stability, moderate income growth and structural reform

43

to meet our objectives, especially in relation to employment.

The national programmes are themselves institutional mechanisms, but the spirit of partnership has also been nourished, both in analysis and action, by other institutional arrangements. Three are particularly important. First, the National Economic and Social Council (NESC) has played a crucial role in developing a shared understanding of the challenge of pursuing economic growth and employment. It has also provided clues about the type of national level partnership arrangements which would work. Second, we have a Central Review Committee (CRC) which brings government and the social partners together to monitor progress on commitments made and to continue dialogue during implementation. Thirdly, and crucially, a new National Economic and Social Forum (NESF) has broadened the range of participants in dialogue and in the partnership process. In particular, the NESF has brought the 'third strand' of the community and voluntary sector directly into the process of analysis and policy development.

National-level partnership cannot be taken for granted, and there are signs that we will have to learn new ways of developing it in the future. That will depend, in particular, on retaining the capacity for shared analysis of the problems which face us and on our being able to demonstrate equitable outcomes for the various parties to national programmes, including government. We need to nourish a broader base of consensus if national programmes are to retain their vigour and we need to move on from the purely national level of agreement to other forms of partnership including, crucially, partnership at firm level as companies face increasing challenges from globalisation. Partnership structures must be able to identify and pursue sources of competitive advantage in an ever more challenging economic environment.

Partnership at local level

Over recent years we have also been attempting to develop and implement a partnership approach to local development in tackling the problems of long-term unemployment. In 1991 (under the PESP), 12 area partnership companies were established on a pilot basis. These focused on tackling long-term unemployment through engaging not only the social partners and state agencies, but also the communities directly involved (see Sarah Craig's paper). The objective was to make such communities the subjects rather than the objects of their own development. Local development based on partnership is now a central element of our Community Support Framework agreement with the European Commission. As such, it will remain a central element in directing the use of structural funds over the next few years.

The central principle we have applied in developing the partnership approach at local level is participation, the active engagement by communities in their own local economic development. We have tried to develop the principle of real partnership where each of the three legs of the partnership stool (communities, social partners and statutory bodies) are given full support, access and respect. And we have tried to emphasise and support a strategic, long-term approach to local development. From that we have put an emphasis on 'multi-dimensionality' or the ability to range widely over issues and programmes which reflect the priorities of communities themselves, rather than the constraints of functional boundaries.

We have also stressed the principle of targeting issues and areas of greatest need. We have placed a strong emphasis on policy learning among local agents of development and at the centre in terms of the funding, delivery and evaluation of mainstream programmes. We have tried to emphasise flexibility as a core value in the local development process, especially on the part of statutory agencies which have perhaps been accustomed to a more hierarchical direction in the past.

In seeking to give a reality to these principles we have been reasonably successful in developing mechanisms to underpin our commitment to local development through partnership. While activity is fundamentally local, there is a vital need for linkages back to the centre because if the centre is fully engaged with the process, it must pick up signals about what needs to be done in terms of mainstream policy and funding.

We have identified, and constructively used, financial incentives. There is no doubt that financial opportunities lubricate the process of dialogue; nothing brings people together better than the prospect of access to funding. From that initial, perhaps rather base beginning, they can move on to genuine multi-disciplinary working between sectors, agencies and disciplines.

We have promoted integration through contracts; not necessarily financial contracts, but clear undertakings on the part of agencies, community groups and social partners, based on their commitment to a strategic plan. For example, in the training area we have had the development of framework agreements between partnerships and training agencies under which community priorities are reflected in targets and evaluation indicators. We have also emphasised delegation, particularly for the statutory agencies, giving local actors and managers the authority and responsibility to respond to the priorities of local partnerships.

Shared challenges

The challenges for partnerships in support of local development are immense. There is the challenge of building links between the structures of representative democracy and the newly emerging structures of participative democracy. There are tensions between elected politicians and community activists and between statutory agencies and local government. Among the social partners there are competing agendas too. There is the challenge of retaining a clear focus on tackling long-term unemployment and dealing with social exclusion. It is easy to be diverted onto other easier tasks, particularly as evaluation mechanisms can prioritise measures of success which are most easy to measure above those which best measure performance against strategic goals. And there is the final challenge of retaining the link between local development partnership and the reinforcement of national level partnership. This is a crucial element in the vitality of the partnership process.

These challenges won't be met lightly. But the potential of the partnership process at local level to respond to the challenge of dislocation from the established structures of governments has been striking. For societies far less troubled than Northern Ireland, obtaining the support and commitment of citizens is an important issue.

In conclusion, our experience suggests that the partnership

process is a critical element in securing the continuing vitality of civil society which, in turn, is the bedrock of democracy. Partnership is also a crucial basis for learning; policy learning, economic learning and learning to trust. In a public administration setting we have learnt lessons that economists have been drawing over recent years from their studies of the most successful and dynamic regions of Europe and the world. The sources of competitive advantage are no longer access to raw materials, markets, or even to new technology. Real competitive advantage comes from the ability to learn and innovate, to interact fruitfully, and to share trusting relationships between suppliers and consumers, between rivals and sectors.

Finally I think we have learned that partnership is about recognising that we have a shared burden to take responsibility, not only for our own sector, but for national and local strategic priorities. The partnership process is ultimately about providing a mechanism by which people can exercise that shared responsibility and move forward with clear vision, a strategic direction and a sense of achievement. While it would be premature to argue that the experience in the Republic proves that the partnership process meets this challenge, there are encouraging signs that it is worth pursuing.

Partnership for Peace and Regeneration

Sir David Fell KCB

Sir David Fell is Head of the Northern Ireland Civil Service.

Partnerships are a means to an end rather than an end in themselves. They offer the opportunity to address shared concerns but they are not an easy option, nor do they carry any guarantee of success. They focus on the responsibilities we have to each other: responsibilities for bringing about positive change; responsibilities brought about by change; and responsibilities which result from the desirable transfer of power from those who have it to those who do not have it yet.

Each sector, whether private, public, voluntary or community, has something distinctive to contribute to a partnership. Skills and knowledge cross sectors, but each sector has a different emphasis and a different culture. Culture can be defined as 'the way we do things around here', and there is no doubt things are done differently in different organisations and sectors. But, at its best, partnership helps us to bring the best from each partner to achieve common goals. That requires compromise, and seeking compromise inevitably brings difficulties.

The Government's strategy for the support of the voluntary sector and community development in Northern Ireland was set out in a document published in 1993. It stated clearly the Government's commitment to working in partnership with the voluntary and community sectors, and it enshrined the Government's view of the value, capacity and diversity of that sector. The strategy emphasised the creative energy and scope for innovation which the voluntary sector could offer.

Partnership is, by definition, a two-way street. It requires good communications and mutual support. In government we particularly value the detailed and considered comments which the voluntary sector has made in consultation exercises, and the expertise which they bring to the policy making process.

Contractual partnerships

Throughout the public services we are now seeing contractual partnerships between sectors; a mixed economy in which the richness of the voluntary and private sectors are brought into areas previously seen as the exclusive daily work of the statutory services.

The involvement in partnership between the statutory and voluntary sectors and community groups has brought us such projects as the excellent 'Home From Hospital Scheme' which gives practical support to people in the home after they have returned from hospital. This project was spearheaded by Bryson House in partnership with the statutory health and social services and there has been very positive feedback from those who have benefited from the scheme. It has also brought us the Princess Royal Trust's partnership for carers involving ten projects which support carers across Northern Ireland. It has brought us the Brownlow Community Trust, funded under the EU Poverty III Programme, and now sustained by local community and statutory agencies working together collaboratively.

There are also scores of community-based initiatives dedicated to the process of peace and regeneration throughout the towns, villages, and border communities of Northern Ireland. These are sponsored by the Department of the Environment, the International Fund for Ireland, and the British and Irish Governments. The Community Regeneration and Improvements Special Programme (CRISP) and the Community Economic Regeneration Scheme (CERS) encourage local groups to come together on a cross-community basis to improve their areas. CRISP is for smaller towns and villages in the designated disadvantaged areas outside Derry and Belfast. CERS aims to encourage local communities in the most deprived parts of larger towns to become involved in developing their own areas to meet needs which the private sector is not meeting.

In Belfast, five projects have been approved since 1988. Outside Belfast 40 CRISP and nine CERS schemes have been approved, with government providing £30 million of the £68 million total investment. Partnerships between government and the community have helped to promote and stimulate economic activity, and have facilitated improvements in the physical environment of smaller towns and villages, making them more attractive to residents, potential investors and visitors. Partnerships have also brought about confidence, civic pride and morale within the local community, as well as a sense of ownership of what has been achieved.

These very positive experiences have been mirrored in the Department of Agriculture's Rural Development Programme which has been successful in helping to create a vibrant rural society through co-operation and partnership between public, private, voluntary and community sectors. That is why the partnership approach was a central element of the Government's rural strategy which was launched in 1994. The philosophy underlying the Rural Development Programme is that rural communities are themselves best placed to identify their needs and propose solutions. Government has worked in partnership with rural community groups to bring forward a total of 34 regeneration projects. In the period up to 1999, it is anticipated that these partnership-based initiatives will bring an injection of £25 million of public funds into rural areas. This would lever a total investment of over £50 million. The economic value of those partnerships lies in the significant number of new job opportunities, businesses and projects being brought into the most disadvantaged rural areas of Northern Ireland.

The social value of partnerships and regeneration projects is of equal importance to the economic value. The social and cultural fabric of communities is improved through the enhanced self confidence and personal ambition created by the success of plans which communities themselves have put together and taken ownership of.

Area partnerships

In Belfast, Making Belfast Work (MBW) will continue to have a key role. In 1994 MBW undertook an extensive consultation on its future strategy. It was probably the most extensive consultation ever undertaken by a public sector body in Northern Ireland. Its core recommendation was the creation of area partnerships involving the councils, the community sector, private industry and the statutory sector. The idea won very broad consensus and the revised MBW strategy launched last year included a commitment to create a number of partnerships throughout Belfast. We already have the Greater Shankill Partnership and a shadow partnership in place covering east Belfast. In the west of the city there is intensive debate about the precise nature of the partnership arrangements. Similar discussions are taking place in north and south Belfast.

Area partnerships have also emerged in a number of areas of Derry. These enable government to take a more strategic approach to targeting social need in the city. Partnerships are involved in a number of key regeneration initiatives such as the Londonderry Regeneration Initiative, also known as Making Derry Work, and various European programmes.

A city Partnership Board was established in Derry last year and another will be established in Belfast this year. They involve a cross section of political, voluntary and community representatives, along with trade unionists and business people. With the widest possible community participation, these bodies are to develop a strategic vision for the city. The challenge is to envisage collectively the sort of city which people want to see in 25 years time. These partnerships are an expression of belief in the future of the community and an understanding that, by establishing their own agenda, citizens can shape public policy and future investment. They are based on the belief that cities belong to the people who inhabit them and that their futures lie in their own hands. These partnerships are therefore a manifestation of communities not simply waiting for changes to happen, but deciding how those changes will happen and making them happen.

The EU special support programme for peace and reconciliation for Northern Ireland and the border counties of Ireland picks up the theme of partnership and emphasises the involvement of local groups and communities. The programme aims to reinforce progress towards a peaceful and stable society, and to promote reconciliation. There is scope in many of the programme's measures for local groups and organisations to work together. The social inclusion sub-programme is key to the whole programme and aims to promote pathways to reconciliation by encouraging grassroots and cross-community co-operation. It places particular emphasis on the development of local community capacities to address neighbourhood problems, and to work in partnership with statutory agencies to develop new and innovative approaches to combating social exclusion.

Innovative delivery

Other partnerships will be developed through the innovative delivery mechanisms of the peace programme. Several parts of the programme will be administered by the intermediary funding bodies, independent of government. These bodies will be working closely with local groups and communities on the ground to identify worthwhile projects and ideas, and to assist groups in bringing their ideas to fruition. Particular consideration will be placed on involving and working with local organisations and local communities. These will not be formal partnerships as such but informal groupings which will come together in a constructive way for the good of the whole community.

Another innovative feature of the Northern Ireland part of the programme is the partnerships sub-programme which involves the creation of formal district partnerships working in conjunction with the Northern Ireland Partnership Board. The district partnerships are to agree a common peace-building vision for their area and support sustainable social and economic development programmes which will have a positive impact on the relations within and between traditionally divided communities. The intention is that this will contribute to a more stable and permanent peace.

Partnership may have come late to Northern Ireland but it is now very firmly embedded. We will undoubtedly see more partnerships developing. We will want to refine our ideas and practices in the light of growing experience and confidence. This cannot but prepare for the partnerships which will be required in a final political accommodation in Northern Ireland. Indeed, that will be necessary if we are to underpin what is still our major shared aim for the future, a Northern Ireland at peace with itself.

A View from Europe

Colin Wolfe

*Colin Wolfe is the Brussels-based European Social Fund
co-ordinator with responsibility for the EU Peace and
Reconciliation Fund for Northern Ireland and the border
counties of the Republic of Ireland. He has particular
responsibility for social inclusion and partnership within
the programme. In this paper, he outlines some of the
background to, and objectives of, the EU programme.
He also gives some insights into European understanding of,
and concern for, the Irish situation.*

In her paper, Maggie Bierne talks of the high-flown language of the
EU programme for peace and reconciliation. This is rather a European thing. The French and others are quite wedded to this kind of
language and, to an English speaker, it can seem a little over the top.
But it is useful because once the high-flown ideals are written down
in black and white, it is possible to wave them in front of officials and
other people involved in the implementation of this programme.
Reminding them of those ideals can often be very useful in pushing
home the things you want to do.

The other point on the European level is that there is a very genuine European interest in this programme. I can think of a number
of reasons for that interest, but one of the main ones is that the idea
of the European community was rooted in the desire to prevent conflict in Europe at the end of the second world war. For the first 50
years of this century Europe was a mess, and one of the achievements of the European Union has been that conflicts have been curtailed. But there was a feeling that the conflict in Northern Ireland
remained a running scar in Europe. With the cease-fire came the
hope that this problem could finally be put to rest, and that hope con-
tinues.

There is also a genuine European interest in - and knowledge of -
the situation in Ireland. Culturally, the Irish both north and south
have a talent for going out, meeting people and developing relationships with them. People on the mainland of Europe are impressed by

that. They get on well with the Irish and have affection for them. One thing they cannot work out is why these wonderful people have so many problems getting on with each other!

Europe with its different nations, regions and points of view, can bring a wider perspective, very much outside the bilateral attitudes that can cause so much trouble. Also, mainland Europeans have a better idea of social partnership and solidarity and the idea of partnership comes naturally to a European programme.

Social inclusion

When the European peace programme was first conceived, it emphasised the economic development aspects. Then input from trade unions, community groups and voluntary groups injected the importance of social inclusion as a central objective in itself, rather than a by-product of economic development. Social inclusion became an important part of the programme following the input from these groups at a conference in Northern Ireland in March 1995. It is important to realise the influence that debate had on the way that the programme was drawn up, and the way that it will be implemented. First, it meant that social inclusion became a separate - and the biggest - sub-programme in the overall initiative. That is very important because the budget reflects priorities as well as having obvious practical effects. As a result of the input at that conference, there was a very significant shift in the way the programme was put together. The idea of social inclusion began to inform the whole philosophy of the programme in a way that was not the case before. It became the single biggest philosophical influence in this programme.

The second thing that has to be underlined about this programme is the theme of decentralisation. Approximately 60 per cent of the funding is decentralised, and that is certainly a big change. It represents a step towards the theme of empowerment through partnership.

It is also important to note the trade union involvement in the programme. Trade unionists were influential in shaping the programme. They are also represented on the district partnerships and on the partnership boards. Trade unionists will, therefore, remain actively involved in the implementation of the programme. On top of the usual monitoring committees, the programme has also introduced a new idea; the consultative forum. The idea is to give everyone involved an opportunity to get together and flag up issues that concern them and have these dealt with as part of the programme. Trade unionists will again play an important part in that forum.

On a more general point, the programme perhaps offers the opportunity to do new and different things. European programmes can often be interpreted in a flexible way, sometimes with quite interesting results. There are possibilities to push ideas to limits and areas that have not previously been thought of and it is certainly worth thinking about the areas where that might be considered.

Getting moving

The thinking behind the programme is that it is better to do things properly than to rush the money out, despite the obvious need to get things moving. There is an imperative to get action started so that the benefits of the cease-fire quickly become more obvious to people on the ground. But it is also important to make sure that the action is happening in the right way.

Some of the centralised intermediary funding bodies have already started to fund projects, the Northern Ireland Voluntary Trust in particular. In March they are touring the area with information so that people are aware of exactly what is on offer, what will be funded, how the decisions will be taken and how to apply for funding. The idea is that applications can be processed by the end of April.

We are talking about very much the same time scale with regard to the government departments. Indeed, one of the welcome things about this programme is the fact that there has been good co-ordination between the government departments, and between their spending and that of the intermediary funding bodies.

District partnerships represent smaller amounts of funding but they are the most important in terms of process because they involve so many people and will get people talking to each other in a way that may not have been emphasised before. The district partnerships will be approved very shortly and then they will get to work. It will take a bit of time before they get to the stage were they are actually funding people, but that should occur by the summer.

In conclusion I want to address two fears which have emerged about the European funding. The first is in response to the obvious question of how the end of the cease-fire will influence the funding. I have to be very clear about that: It will not influence the flow of funding. Even if the situation went back to the worst of the pre-cease-fire times, the spending would still go ahead. The themes of peace and reconciliation remain just as important whether there is a cease-fire or not. Indeed, it might be argued that they are even more important in the absence of a cease-fire.

The second point is that this money is genuinely additional. All European money has to go on top of existing spending but it would be particularly wrong if this money were not unequivocally additional. This money was dredged out of all corners of the European budget by the European tax payer. Its wasn't programmed. It wasn't expected. But they put together this package. It would be quite wrong if that money was not spent on the aims and the objectives that the tax payers have set.

Local Responses to Cross-Border Co-operation

James Corrigan

James Corrigan is a Research Fellow at the Institute of European Studies at Queen's University, Belfast. This paper is based on a preliminary study of the EU INTERREG programmes and the EU Initiative for Peace and Reconciliation

This paper draws on a research project recently completed at Queen's University and subsequent research in the border region. The research focused on the impact of European integration and local cross-border co-operation on the socio-economic regeneration and development of the border areas. In designating the study area, the project took into account the variety of official definitions of the border area (including by the European Union (EU) and the International Fund for Ireland), balanced against local definitions. The study area included all county and district councils areas contiguous to the border plus Down District Council area which was included because of the Council's long-standing involvement in cross border co-operation and its leading role in the East Border Region Committee.

The economy of the region

Our analysis, which draws on surveys of border residents and councillors, semi-structured interviews with large numbers of key participants and a socio-economic report, demonstrates the development problems of the border region. The region lacks coherent functional identity (a limited form of identity has been institutionalised in the southern border counties by the establishment of a Border Region Authority for structural fund purposes but no such regional grouping exists in the north). It has few natural resources or large towns, and it has a highly dispersed population of over 800,000, or 16 per cent of the island's total population. Its peripheral situation has distanced it from the main centres of economic activity and political decision-making.

Overall, the region has lower incomes, higher rates of unemployment (including long-term unemployment) and higher dependency ratios than other regions. The previous census figures show 20 per cent unemployment in the Northern Ireland border region, five per cent above the figure for the Northern Ireland as a whole. The level of unemployment in the Republic of Ireland border region is three per cent higher than the rest of the Republic (see graph below). The border areas also have higher levels of long-term unemployment than their non-border counterparts. In the Northern Ireland border area, 39 per cent of those unemployed had been unemployed for over two years, compared to 34 per cent in the rest of Northern Ireland. The corresponding figures in the Republic are 31 per cent and 27 per cent respectively. There are also variations between and within council areas in the border region (see tables 1 and 2).

In areas where overall unemployment is relatively low, wards with high unemployment still exist. In areas of high unemployment, some wards are particularly disadvantaged (see table 2). For example, the Brandywell ward in Derry has 50 per cent unemployment. It is important that policies and funding not only develop the border region generally, but also respond to the' internal' variations of marginalisation and exclusion.

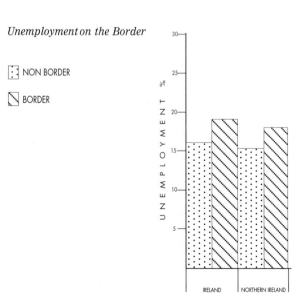

Unemployment on the Border

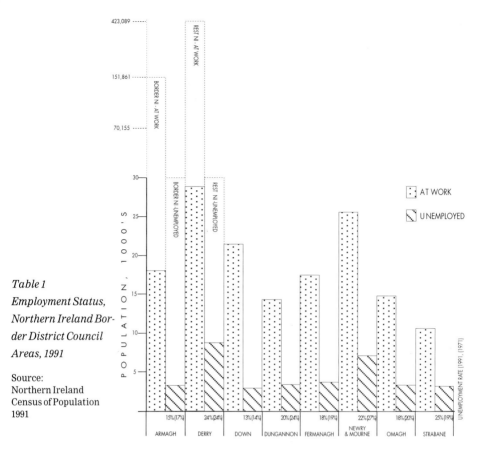

Table 1

Employment Status, Northern Ireland Border District Council Areas, 1991

Source:
Northern Ireland Census of Population 1991

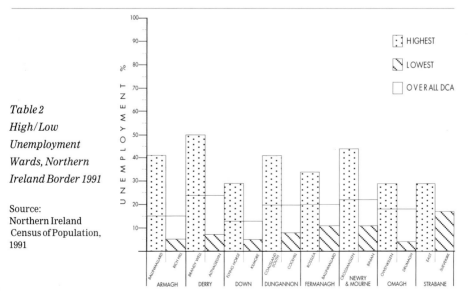

Table 2

High/Low Unemployment Wards, Northern Ireland Border 1991

Source:
Northern Ireland Census of Population, 1991

Regenerating the Border Region

The special problems of the Irish border region, including the high level of unemployment, were first documented by the EU in a 1983 report. It said the socio-economic disadvantages of the area were compounded by the frontier which "restricts scope for development and trade". Until the 1980s there was little formalised cross-border co-operation apart from limited developments such as the Foyle Fisheries Commission and the Erne Catchment Area Scheme.

Over the past decade, there has been a major influx of funds - mainly from the EU - to tackle the development problems of the wider cross-border region. In addition to the EU structural funds, the region has received special assistance from the INTERREG initiative which has the twin objectives of developing the border region and encouraging cross-border co-operation. Between 1991 and 1993, INTERREG I contributed over UK£60 million. INTERREG II, which runs from 1994 to 1999, will contribute £122 million. In addition, the International Fund for Ireland has contributed £290 million across Northern Ireland and the border counties since 1986. The present EU initiative for peace and reconciliation has earmarked £240 million for a three year period (1995-1997). Overall investment has also been increased by the availability of matching funds from government and the private sector.

With the availability of these funds and the improved opportunities for tackling the problems of the region, there are a number of specific questions that need to be addressed. What type of political and administrative framework is most conducive to socio-economic regeneration and cross-border co-operation? Do present frameworks facilitate social inclusion? What is the extent of democratic accountability?

Political and administrative framework

A number of local organisations have said that the way programmes are implemented is at least as important as their stated objectives. Local responses from the Irish border region suggest that existing political and administrative structures were inadequate for the implementation of the first INTERREG programme and may actually have hindered the development of local cross-border economic co-operation. A wide section of local opinion said that INTERREG was too centralised and they wished to see more accessible administration. A Louth TD claimed that the two governments' finance departments have "an incredibly partitionist attitude with respect to structural funds and INTERREG."

The official evaluation of INTERREG I said that the Irish programme had more genuine' cross-border projects that other objective one' border regions in the EU. However, our research in the region indicated that only a small number of cross-border projects were funded and that a number of high profile projects, such as the Erne-Shannon link, received the bulk of the funds. Indeed, the EU Court of Auditors has recently said that "many actions bore little relation to the specifically cross-border vocation of INTERREG" and that "only 39 of the 270 projects of INTERREG I were of a transfrontier nature and were receiving joint financing from the two member states of that basis." The European Commission defended the Irish programme saying that the land frontier in Ireland presented particular political and administrative difficulties.

There have been a number of changes under INTERREG II. Both finance departments have consulted more widely and local responses are reflected in the new programme. An INTERREG development officer has been appointed to promote the programme at local level and provide practical assistance to local groups, organisations and individuals. However, the management of the programme through implementation, monitoring and evaluation rests with the two government departments - a structure that is defended by their experiences of joint administration under the previous programme. There is only a limited monitoring role at regional level.

The administrative structure for the EU peace and reconciliation initiative has attempted to address the many criticisms of INTERREG. The EU task force set up to examine the objectives and administration of this initiative were guided that "monitoring and management arrangements should build on the experience with cross-border programmes under INTERREG." They also sought structures that would promote reconciliation, boost economic growth and extend social inclusion.

It is in this context that a partial decentralisation of the peace programme has been introduced where a number of intermediary funding bodies, independent of government, have been delegated responsibility for bringing development closer to the grassroots. The incorporation of the principle of area or district partnerships is also a significant development as its seeks more participative models of local economic development. The new partnerships represent a decentralisation of certain responsibilities to the local level while providing a mechanism for the inclusion of local elected representatives, community and voluntary groups, representatives from the private sector and other interests. The culture of partnership appears to be more developed south of the border where the social partners are represented on the EU monitoring committees.

Do these new structures represent a more effective means of local socio-economic regeneration and cross-border economic co-operation? The view from local level is generally positive, although there is some caution. Could the addition of area partnerships and intermediary bodies to the existing structures lead to a lack of co-ordination and fragmentation of initiatives at local level? There are presently a number of organisations which overlap in functional and geographical remits and, in some cases, membership. This fear was expressed by the Border Region Authority in its submission to the peace programme. It referred to a "crowded landscape" and advocated a decentralised structure but minimal addition to existing administrative structures.

Social inclusion

The second question on social inclusion is itself closely related to the administrative structures of the funding programmes and is a vital programme objective in its own right within the peace programme. The peace programme aims "to promote pathways to reconciliation by encouraging grassroots and cross-community co-operation, especially in the most deprived areas in Northern Ireland and the border counties, as well as action to address the specific difficulties faced by vulnerable groups and others at a disadvantage such as victims, children, young people and those previously caught up with violence including prisoners and ex-prisoners."

The wider consultation under INTERREG, and particularly the peace programme, provided greater opportunities for marginalised groups and individuals to express their needs and aspirations and thus shape the programme. However, social inclusion must go beyond consultation and specific measures to tackle marginalisation and exclusion from decision-making. It is imperative that political and administrative structures should facilitate access to the decision-making process for those marginalised in society.

Our research, on INTERREG in particular, demonstrated the problems faced by many groups and communities in carrying out a project, especially a cross-border project. These problems, which are most common in marginalised communities, include lack of information on funding programmes, lack of technical assistance, bureaucracy (particularly for cross-border projects) and matching funds. On the latter point, the Combat Poverty Agency recently said the requirement that groups contribute 25 per cent towards the cost of a project is restrictive for many community and voluntary groups. "If socially excluded groups already had 25 per cent matching funding' available, they would no longer be excluded," it said. The peace programme allows governments discretion on this issue.

Democratic accountability
Many of our non-elected interviewees felt that practical cross-border co-operation and economic regeneration was best achieved by circumventing politicians and the divisions they represented. This non-political approach was frequently advocated by officials, business people and local community and voluntary groups. Indeed, a number of groups stressed their non-political nature as a means of acting as intermediaries in the dispersal of funds.

However, this also raises the issue of democratic accountability and the role of locally elected representatives. Local authorities are taking an increasingly active role in economic development but are limited by their relative lack of powers. In addition, cross-border economic development between councils is limited by the mismatch of responsibilities and priorities. There is the added difficulty of political differences about what the extent and scope of cross-border co-operation should be. However, our research has indicated general support for increased cross-border economic co-operation and this is reflected in new and strengthened cross-border partnerships between county and district councils. The new area and district partnerships are well placed to further socio-economic regeneration through cross-community and cross-border co-operation.

Section Four
Community Development and Partnership in Practice

Power and Partnership in the 'Real World'

Maureen Gaffney

*Maureen Gaffney is Chairperson of the National Economic
and Social Forum (NESF) which was established by the
Irish Government in 1993 to contribute to the national consensus on economic and social policy. Membership of the
Forum is drawn from government and opposition parties,
the social partners and a 'third strand' representing groups
including the unemployed and disadvantaged, women,
people with disabilities, young people, the elderly and
environmental groups. Developing strategies to combat
unemployment is an important part of its work. This paper
originally formed part of Ms Gaffney's summing up of the
joint IMPACT-UNISON conference.*

The National Economic and Social Forum (NESF) consists of 49
people. One third are elected representatives; TDs from all political parties in government and opposition. Another third is made up
of the social partners (employers' organisations, unions and farmers' representatives). The third strand is made up of the voluntary
and community sector.

What's in it for me?
The key issue in partnership-building is relationship-building and
that is intensely psychological territory. Throughout the papers in
this book, contributors write of trust as a critical issue in partnership-building. Trust is often seen as a prerequisite to good partnership. But you don't need trust at the beginning; indeed, you can't
have trust at the beginning because there is no basis for it. All you
need at the beginning is a working relationship and to be open to the

idea that you can work towards trusting relationships. Trust has to be preceded by a much more cautious and measured interaction; an approached characterised by the question 'what is in this for me?'

For those without power, it is very obvious what is in partnership to them - a sense of commitment, of being included in something worthwhile, a sense of control over their destiny, and a sense of being supported by others. But what is in it for those who already have power? Why should they be interested in partnerships? One reason that people who already have power will go into partnerships is if they believe it will make their life easier. In other words, partnerships offer possibilities if they allow peoples' goals to be met in different ways. That is why people on statutory bodies or social partners are interested in going into more expanded partnership arrangements.

Risk and responsiveness

The 'what's in it for me?' phase is a cautious stand-off and will remain that way until one party in the partnership is prepared to take a risk and put its own self-interest on the back burner for the sake of responding to the partner. Responsiveness is the key to building trust in partnerships. Partnership is not about 'doing good', doing what you think is the right thing to do. Rather, it is responding to what the other person needs, as they see it. Unless that risk is taken - and it is a risk - a partnership never goes beyond the *quid pro quo* stage.

If that responsiveness is reciprocated, there is an upward spiral of trust and then the relationship-building phase of the partnership can really begin. It is only in that second phase that the partnership can develop its capacity to deal with conflict. As trust begins to be established, the question 'what's in it for me?' can be replaced by how can I do business in a way that's good for me but also good for the relationship between us?

Once you reach that stage, you need to maximise all parties' partnership skills in areas like team-working and decision-making. The ability to communicate properly becomes critical. Not simply an exchange of views but an empathic communication where you listen to someone and actually care about what they say. The critical element in partnership is to understand your partner's position, and only then have your own positions understood. That approach pays unquantifiable dividends.

Being 'bilingual' about power

This raises two different ways of working which are underpinned by two different versions of power. Traditionally the idea of power is based on hierarchies with very rigid roles and rules. But the community and voluntary sector brings a very different idea of power. They are characterised by flatter hierarchies, participative democracy and full involvement and that often means long discussions before anything can be agreed.

These different ideas of power require partnerships to be 'bilingual' about power. To get things moving within the limits of time, money and patience, you need a more traditional version of power. You need to be able to make decisions quickly and with limited information; you can't involve everybody in everything. On the other hand, without involvement, nothing sticks and nothing is bedded down.

I have always found it interesting that each of the two worlds of power tends to describe itself as coming from the 'real world.' Decision-makers like business people and civil servants will say: 'I have to take real decisions because I am in the real world.' The community people say: 'Look we are living in the real world. We are the people with the real problems.' Both views are equally valid and successful partnership means being able to move in and out of those different ways of thinking, experience and doing business.

Countervailing pressures

The third basic dynamic is the relationship of the individual to the whole which expresses itself in the question 'to what extent am I part of this partnership and to what extent am I separate from it?' Both needs - to be part of it yet separate from it - have to be honoured in all partnerships and different groups have different ways of resolving that basic dilemma; in a marriage, community, job, or society. There are often countervailing movements. There is the huge creative, cohesive force that comes from being part of a partnership organisation where individuals get to know and like each other. On the other hand, people are under huge amounts of pressure in their own constituencies. People from the community sector have to report back to groups who may be on the look-out for betrayal. People from trade unions or business also have to account to people at another level. Everyone involved in partnerships can come under tremendous pressure from their own constituents.

Finally I come back to the idea of power and what we mean by it. There is a lot of discussion about choice in this book. Choice is the prerogative of the powerful. People who have no power have no choices, because choice implies that all other things are equal. There is no choice if people are being asked to decide between surviving and not surviving. If weaker partners feel they have no choice outside of the partnership terms they are being offered, they will find it almost impossible to do business unless that feeling of powerlessness is understood and dealt with by the other parties.

But we also have to be careful about attributing too much power to other people and too little to ourselves. For example, in a traditional hierarchy of power, people always think power rests with the next layer up. But if you go all the way up the hierarchy, those at the top say: 'We have no real power. All the power is outside with the electorate, lobby groups or with other forces.' The reality is that power does not reside in any one place. It is dispersed and the system of power can be activated anywhere. The important thing is to find ways of exerting leverage in the system. But what if you feel you have no power? Perhaps the really important thing is to realise that you have the power to change yourself, your way of thinking about power, your way of working with power. Once you do that, you are changing the way other people will respond to you.

A Shared Vision

Padraic A White

Since 1991, Padraic White has chaired the Northside Partnership in one of the most economically deprived areas of Dublin. He was formerly chief executive of the Irish Industrial Development Authority of Ireland (IDA) the state agency which encouraged the establishment of over 1,000 foreign companies in the Republic of Ireland.

I would like to start with a quotation from the Bible: "When there is no vision, the people perish". That applies to Dublin's Northside Partnership where 18 people have found themselves around a table as the result of a national formula agreed between government, business, and trade unions. Six are from the trade unions and business community; six are from local authorities and the statutory sector; and six are from the community sector. That mix can only work if there is a vision that binds people together.

Each of the 18 people came to the Northside Partnership with different perceptions, but those perceptions have changed. For example, I used to hear the word 'exploitation' and angry complaints about 'state bureaucracies' around the table. I don't hear that any more; we now speak the same language. The key to that change is that we have a shared vision and our vision is a very simple one.

Inside our heads we have a picture of a bridge. On one side of the bridge is the world of unemployment and welfare dependency. On the other side is the world of work, economic independence and self respect. Very simply, we have defined our job as helping people to cross over the bridge into the world of work. We test everything we do amongst ourselves by asking 'how is this relevant to the job of getting people from one side of the bridge to the other?'

It is easy to lose focus in the partnership business. You could be running community development or child care facilities for everybody in the area. But you must have a filter that tells you how your activity relates to your goal and your vision. For example, we are involved in child care but we have limited our interest to child care to helping the parent or guardian to return to the work force or take up training for employment.

69

Two sets of clients

The second thing we clarified in our own minds is that we simultaneously have two sets of clients. The first is the unemployed. We adopt the philosophy that nobody really understands the problems of the individual unemployed person trying to get into work except themselves. So we have listened, and when we have come across a problem or something we didn't understand, we have responded to it. For example, we found that we sometimes got work for people only to find that they didn't show up on the second day because they had lost the motivation and energy for work. To bridge that gap we developed a 12-week motivation course that deals with the individual, how they feel about themselves, their physical attitude towards themselves, and so on. The content of the motivation course was developed as a result of consultation and dialogue with unemployed people themselves.

Again, we found that many people lacked interview skills. So we set up a simple one-week interview skills course which has been highly successful. We also found that long-term unemployed people had little or no work experience to put on their CV. They were caught in the classic vicious circle where they couldn't get work because they hadn't the experience, but they couldn't get the experience because they had no job. So we have created a commercial subsidiary company (Speedpack Ltd) that does special packaging and other sub-contract work for local industry. With that, we have created six month employment contracts for the long-term unemployed as part of the passage into jobs. In April 1996, some 24 people were on contract work with Speedpack Ltd at normal commercial rates, many of them older unemployed people who usually have great difficulty getting re-started in work.

Business involvement

Our second set of clients is the business community. The involvement of the business community has been the secret to everything we have done in the Northside Partnership. Because no matter what the rest of us do on the welfare side or in training, it all stops at the door of the personnel manager. If we can't get through that door the whole thing collapses.

So, we have involved local industry and we have established a network of 200 companies which use our placement service. More importantly, we have seen a change in the hearts and minds of the business community. They have been prepared to change the rules of recruitment in subtle ways to give unemployed people a chance. That is the secret of the ultimate placement of the long-term unemployed and we are building on it all the time.

Because of the crucial importance of the interface between the job seeker and the company with a job, we set up a specialised contact point to prepare our unemployed clients for work and to put them forward for jobs where we believe they have a high chance of succeeding. The three business representatives on the board of Northside Partnership have given us credibility with local employers and access to them.

From welfare to work

We have a population of 100,000 in our area of which 10,000 are registered unemployed and 37,000 are welfare dependants. We have not set out to be marginal in our impact. We have set ourselves a specific target of placing 4,400 unemployed people in jobs between 1996 and 1999 (inclusive). We have taken on the responsibility for making a serious impact on unemployment in our area. We have consulted widely on our plans and we published a four-year action plan in March 1996.

The Northside Partnership Board seeks to apply sound business practices to its work; clear targets, efficient operating, tight financial control, and realistic and honest evaluation. We believe that the unemployed deserve a businesslike, rather than a woolly-headed, approach. I believe our approach is a credit to all the groups represented on the Partnership Board, particularly FÁS, City of Dublin VEC, the Irish Business and Employers' Confederation and the Irish Congress of Trade Unions.

Partnership Across Communities

Geraldine McAteer

Geraldine McAteer is Manager of the Upper Springfield Trust in Belfast.

The Upper Springfield area is in nationalist west Belfast and includes areas such as Ballymurphy and Turf Lodge. It has an unemployment rate of over 60 per cent. The youth population is over 50 per cent of the total and there is very high youth unemployment. The social and economic problems of the area have been compounded by the violence of the last 25 years; by death, internment, large scale imprisonment and political vetting. As a result, the area has experienced deep-rooted alienation and marginalisation politically, socially and economically.

If you asked me to bet on what would be the last place in west Belfast you would have a partnership between statutory bodies, the private sector and the community, as a Falls Road woman I would have put my money on Ballymurphy and the Upper Springfield area! But we do have a partnership and it is important to ask how and why that happened and how it can empower the community.

Community control
The Upper Springfield Trust was established in 1993 because of a number of factors. Firstly there already existed a vibrant community infrastructure. Over the years, many people in the local neighbourhoods had direct experience of the area's problems and were actively involved in trying to address them. They had clear ideas of what was needed on the ground and were prepared to work hard to follow them up. Secondly, the area benefited from a positive intervention by Making Belfast Work who took a fresh approach to the area and developed a positive agenda for working with local people to affect real change. Thirdly, through Business in the Community, Making Belfast Work involved people from the private sector who brought business and organisational skills into this working class area. The partnership was finally negotiated on terms that allowed full community participation with nine elected community repre-

sentatives on the partnership. Therefore, we had the benefit of the statutory and private sector, but the partnership had full community participation and worked to a community agenda.

Cross-community

A couple of years ago Making Belfast Work drew our attention to the European Commission's URBAN initiative. URBAN's aims are to stimulate social and economic development through a series of projects and physical improvements and, in so doing, to create jobs. Making Belfast Work (MBW) in conjunction with the Trust's other statutory partners, including the North and West Health and Community Trust, suggested that we get together in partnership with the Shankill Partnership in the protestant, unionist area adjacent to ours to put in a joint bid to Europe. A lot of hard work on the part of the two partnerships, including the statutory and business partners, succeeded with the result that £13 million will come into the two areas and be spent on social and economic regeneration programmes.

I have no doubt that we were successful in our bid because it was a joint bid from two communities, involving consultants and backed by MBW. And, because of the way the trusts are comprised in both the areas, the money will be used to empower the local communities to tackle their economic and social problems and add to job creation. Clearly, that is one very good example of where communities can come together in partnership for the benefit of their communities. We now have to submit business plans which will mean involving professionals, but at the end of the day it will be the people of the Shankill and Upper Springfield who will decide how the money is spent.

Becoming friends

Over the last few years the Shankill Partnership, the Forth River Trust and the Foundry Trust in the Falls area have all worked hard to attract inward investment to west Belfast. During the peace process we have taken every opportunity - for example, in our contacts with America - to get as good a deal as we can for our local communities. For example, we jointly hosted the US Commerce Department trade mission to west Belfast where we linked US companies with local west Belfast companies. It was a disappointment that none of the US companies settled in west Belfast, but what we did achieve was a very good working relationship between our communities and with the companies already in west Belfast. That has enabled us jointly to talk to the companies about how we get unemployed people from the Falls and Shankill into jobs.

Because we have worked together, and because we have worked with other agencies, local firms now have a different view of our two communities. They now take our trusts and our community organisations seriously and that will pan out into real jobs for local people.

This has been a very positive relationship for both communities. We have worked together to develop proposals and to get our people into jobs. In the process we have got to know each other personally. It would be naive to think that because we have worked together we will have the same political point of view. But what we have done is to develop friendships. We have got to know each other and we have developed common agendas in terms of our own communities. The bonds made over the last few years will be strong ones. For example, at the March 1996 meeting of the Upper Springfield Trust, one of the first things on the agenda was to seek a meeting with the Shankill partnership to discuss how URBAN was progressing. If we were honest, the purpose was also to say, 'things are bad at the moment but we are still friends, we still have things to talk about.' That is a major spin-off from the partnerships.

*Lagan College Belfast
has pupils from both
communities*

HOMER SYKES/NETWORK

Agree Aims and Objectives

Ann McVicker

Ann McVicker is the Co-ordinator of the Shankill Women's Centre in Belfast. She is also an ICTU representative on the Belfast Partnership Board.

Three years ago none of the community groups in Belfast knew anything about European funding. It was only when information was shared at seminars and conferences that we learned. We are now at the start of another learning process as regards partnerships.

I have experience and knowledge of three types of partnerships. The first is a partnership at the micro-level. Almost two years ago, the Shankill Women's Centre entered into a partnership with Northern and West Belfast Trust. We now work out of the same building and share a lot of resources. There is also a healthy exchange of views, ideas and opinions. The Shankill Women's Centre provides education, child care, information and support for the women and children of the greater Shankill area. In return, the Trust contributes about 23 per cent of our total expenditure.

To date, both partners are getting something out of it but there could be problems in the future which we have not yet come across. There is no strategic plan and no exit strategy, and there is certainly an unequal division of power within the partnership. For instance, if the Trust gave us three months notice to quit, that would be the end of the partnership. If it were a genuine partnership there would be some sort of contractual obligation on the part of the Trust to continue to contribute to our running costs. To date the partnership has worked well because of a good mix of personalities, but there is no solid foundation to the partnership.

The second partnership I have experience of is the Greater Shankill Partnership. This partnership evolved from the Greater Shankill Strategy; it is very much like an urban regeneration partnership. It was the first in Belfast and a lot of the emerging partnerships are based on the Greater Shankill model. Although it is early days yet (there have only been four meetings to date) it has the broad consensus of the greater Shankill community and we see much potential in it.

75

The Greater Shankill partnership has helped to focus the community and develop strategic thinking and planning. It has the potential to reassure communities that their problems are being taken seriously and it has already attracted funding and targeted resources more effectively. But there are pitfalls too, including a lack of communication. It lacks clear aims, objectives or exit strategies, which means problems could be stored up for a later date.

Area partnerships also have the potential to dilute community politics and activism. Some would say that partnership has already marginalised and silenced community groups and workers. Once you are on the partnership track it is hard to get off. If you question and challenge you can be penalised and left to go it alone, unsupported. There are already examples of groups who have put in funding applications and have had to demonstrate that their proposed project comes in line with the strategy or the action plan.

The third partnership I have experience of is a district partnership, Belfast District Shadow Partnership, which is really a vehicle for distributing peace money. This narrow focus could be a lost opportunity because the partnership could be developed into a model for informing local decision-making.

The DoE guidelines should be imposed on district partnerships and adhered to in order to gender-balance the partnerships. The aims and objectives of partnerships should be discussed and agreed from the beginning so that you don't race ahead and ignore the processes necessary for partnerships to evolve and develop. Unless training needs are addressed, lack of training, education and support for all members on partnerships will foster greater inequalities. Codes of conduct and good practice must be accommodating, supportive and inclusive. This could range from councillors improving their manners to the provision of child care and time-tabling of meetings to support members rather than disabling them.

Partnerships are here to stay. There is real potential for different sectors to come together in ways that value and respect each others' contribution. Partnership is not about building on old structures and ways of doing things; its about making the mind-shift. That is a challenge for all of us.

Listen to the Communities

Seamus Heaney

Seamus Heaney is the Community Programme Facilitator in Creggan Neighbourhood Partnership in Derry

The European structural fund special support programme for peace and reconciliation places particular emphasis on 'social inclusion' and 'partnership' as key philosophical objectives. Emphasis is also placed on decentralised funding as a step towards community empowerment.

There is a perception that because of their lack of business experience, community organisations might squander this opportunity. But it is wrong to suppose that, because community groups have relatively little business experience, they are not capable of using development funding in a realistic and responsible way. It is true that community groups have had little or no experience of business in the past, but a business acumen is not the be-all and end-all of addressing community needs. Furthermore, business developments have been taking place in many disadvantaged communities and community business is thriving.

In Creggan, a community business has very successfully developed a retail and community enterprise centre which has created a new social and economic heart in the community. Services which should have been in place many years ago have come from the efforts of the community itself, with financial support from the International Fund for Ireland and the DoE. The idea that community groups would squander money implies that they are not capable of identifying their own needs or determining how they would use money and resources to address those needs.

The peace package will be administered through seven intermediary bodies and 27 district partnerships. The total funding will be in the region of £240 million. It is a substantial sum of money, but one which is in danger of being spread so thinly that its impact in areas of most need will be negligible. I am concerned that the peace and reconciliation funding is being packaged in such comparatively small amounts that it will be difficult for neighbourhood partnerships to access substantial sums of money for strategic community development.

Creggan Neighbourhood Partnership is still evolving as a partnership and we have not yet involved statutory bodies or the private sector. The local community groups are the core members and we have agreed 'our' vision. The partnership has recently published a report into poverty and deprivation in the Creggan area. *Meeting Local Needs Through Partnership* argues that the key areas of investment must reflect the priority needs of the community. A copy of the report will be delivered to every household in the community so that the community itself will know what is going on and can criticise and comment on the proposals.

Having identified needs, we are now looking to determine what type of partnership we are going to have. I tend to be a bit suspicious when government and statutory bodies get enthusiastic about partnership. In the context of neighbourhood partnerships, statutory bodies are not so much of the partnership; the partnership is essentially between local people and those involved in the community and voluntary sector who service the needs of communities.

There is also a growing suspicion that money coming in from the EU peace and reconciliation fund may simply be replacing money cut from the budgets of statutory bodies. Tens of millions of pounds are being withdrawn or withheld by the British Government in the current financial year. I wonder, if you added all the sums of money cut from the budgets of different statutory bodies in the north of Ireland, would it add up to around about £240 million? I have a sneaking suspicion that it might.

There is a feeling that the concept of partnership and the intended use of the peace and reconciliation budget is more about covering the losses in mainstream budgets than it is about involving people in new ways of governing communities. If that is what is meant by partnerships, the answer is 'no!' Communities are not going to be used in this way. If partnerships are about anything, they are about people making genuine commitments to one another. First and foremost there must be a commitment to care, and to respect each others' views. The statutory bodies may not be *of* the partnership but they must commit themselves *to* the partnership. They must be prepared to respect our views and they must be prepared to provide local communities and partnerships with the necessary resources to address our problems.

Training First - Funding Later

Ann Graham

Ann Graham is the co-ordinator of a small community-based women's centre on the Ballybean estate in Belfast.

Ballybean is the second largest estate in Northern Ireland, with over 2,500 houses. Like many outlying estates Ballybean is characterised by lack of social, health and other support services and facilities. There is a high dependency on benefits, high unemployment, low academic achievement and a high incidence of lone parents.

Some years ago, before the term partnership came into vogue, an attempt was made to bring the major statutory and voluntary organisations together to develop a strategy to address some of these problems. This Housing Executive initiative had some success. With no budget, its success depended on the level of commitment each of the statutory bodies brought to it. The key problems included the lack of co-ordination of services by the statutory and voluntary sector, and a lack of recognition and understanding of the community and voluntary sector and the valuable contribution it makes.

Partnerships should address problems like poor community infrastructure and development, the absence of funding policies and accessing core funding from statutory organisations, which has been made more difficult by the purchaser-provider split in the health and social services, and by the contracting out of services.

I hope that partnerships will be an opportunity for greater understanding and recognition for the contribution the community sector makes and an opportunity to influence statutory and private agencies to provide more responsive and relevant services. I hope it brings greater inter-agency co-operation and better representation of women on partnership boards.

There are opportunities, but I also have a number of fears. There is a vast difference of understanding of working in partnership and consultation between the statutory sector and the community sector. There has always been a sense that the under-funded and under-resourced community sector is an unequal partner. There is suspicion of the different agendas each sector brings to the partnership and a fear that partnerships are really only creating another tier of bureaucracy which could exclude small local community organisations and local initiatives which do not necessarily comply with the broader strategy. There are also questions of representation and accountability, and the relationships between the various partnerships that are being set up.

Of the 22 people currently sitting on the Greater East Belfast Shadow Partnership, only four are women. Of them, three are community representatives and the other is from the statutory sector. It was extremely disappointing that councils in particular didn't make more of an effort to nominate women onto the partnership.

The partnership has been in existence for nine months and the fact that it has no funding role yet has given us some space to concentrate on the process of partnerships and the development of mechanisms to ensure more open communication with the community and greater participation by a wider number of individuals.

There is a need to slow up the funding process until there has been better training in areas like PAFT and TSN (see Maggie Bierne's paper). The DOE guidelines say that departments should use all appropriate measures at their disposal to ensure that non-departmental public bodies comply with PAFT and TSN. I would be very interested to know what those measures are and how they are going to be implemented. There is a need for training, not only for the community representatives but for all the representatives, on the issues of PAFT and TSN so that they can start from a firm base.

JUSTIN LEIGHTON/NETWORK

Partnerships Must Support Community Interests

Eileen Howell

Eileen Howell is the Director of the Falls Community Council in Belfast.

The Falls Community Council operates in a strongly nationalist and republican area of west Belfast. The Falls has a history of marginalisation and alienation and its community has been excluded from power structures over generations. One recent Secretary of State referred to it as a 'terrorist community.'

In the 1970s, community development flourished in west Belfast, mainly on a voluntary basis. This is now held up as a model to other communities which are trying to strengthen their local community infrastructure. Community development in west Belfast had two functions. Firstly it developed radical policy responses and strategies which challenged government policy and intervention in the area. Secondly, it became an alternative to political and civic inclusion.

The emergence of the partnership model as a new mechanism to deliver regeneration in west Belfast presents new working relationships which will challenge past perceptions and experiences of government departments and the statutory sector. The responsibility for building new relationships must rest with both the community sector and public officials. The new arrangements will mean working with bodies which have treated us differently in the past and have, in many senses, been perceived as the 'enemy'. This powerful dimension to setting up the partnership model in west Belfast should not be underestimated.

The west Belfast community's contribution to the cease-fire and peace process was set out in the document *Clar Nua*. This set out a vision for the future covering ten key policy areas, all underpinned by human and civil rights, TSN and the PAFT guidelines - without which social inclusion and economic justice cannot be achieved.

As we prepare to discuss the many issues raised by the west Belfast partnership - issues which will determine future relationships between the community and the public sector - we have a number of concerns. First of all, many difficulties will be created for the community sector if it enters partnership against the background of ongoing cuts in health care, housing and other social and economic areas. Secondly, a partnership for the regeneration of west Belfast requires a remit for policy and strategic planning which will bring the partnership into conflict with government policy and planning for the area. Thirdly, the partnership will have to develop a broad range of programmes to tackle deprivation.

The community must be fully resourced if it is really to be an equal partner. This requires a commitment to expertise, technical and other assistance from government. The community has mechanisms to ensure representativeness and accountability. By its very nature, the public sector will not be able to ensure the same level of accountability or representativeness.

The partnership must be accountable to the community and must command the respect and support of the people it is supposed to serve. It cannot simply be a mechanism to implement government policy in the area, or rubber-stamp decisions which have a negative impact on the people of west Belfast. If it is, it will be the focus of much anger and frustration as it will undermine the success of local community development in the area over the last 25 years.

Section Five
Views from Public Sector
Employers and Trade Unions

A View from the Statutory Sector

Michael McLoone

Michael McLoone is Donegal County Council Manager in the Republic of Ireland. Before that he was manager of the Beaumont hospital in Dublin and manager for community care services in Donegal, Leitrim and Sligo.

I want to focus on two things. The first relates to the strategies local authorities can adopt to engage people in more participative processes. The second relates to enterprise and county strategies, and county strategy groups.

In the Republic, county councils have a much wider remit than district councils. They are responsible for roads, water supplies, sewage, housing, planning and development, town and village renewal. Donegal County Council has an annual budget of about £43 million (revenue) and £20 million (capital). For the last 18 months we have been working to decentralise the administration of these services into five electoral areas with populations ranging between 14,000 and 27,000.

While partnerships and area-based planning have been very much in vogue, in many places there has been difficulty in defining the logical area for implementation. In Donegal, we take the view that electoral area, where political and administrative boundaries converge, is a good unit. We see the decentralisation of the administration of front-line services to our five area offices as one way to focus on the area as the unit of planning and implementation.

That also means rationalising the deployment of staff, putting road and housing engineers, sanitary services people, planners, town and village renewal people and administrative back-up into the local community. We believe they can then more easily identify with the community and do business with local development groups. Importantly, it also enables us to synchronise with an area-based strategy.

Our approach has the backing of unions, staff and local development groups. Part of our strategy is to involve people in their own communities with the staff who deliver services, and delegate authority to staff in local areas so that decisions can be taken quickly.

As County Manager, I am chairman of the Donegal County Enterprise Board which covers the entire county. I am also a member of a LEADER company which is going to administer an area of partnership. I also work voluntarily with a local group. We are trying to build partnership through an experimental arrangement sponsored by the Enterprise Trust, which we call a 'membership company'. We are inviting the business community, the unemployed and community groups to join as members, to form a membership company as a model for this concept of partnership on the ground.

One of the major challenges confronting us at county level is the problem of integrating strategies both for the county and for areas within it. There is a growing number of agencies with an interest in economic and social development: four LEADER companies and four area partnerships, County Tourism, the County Enterprise Board, as well as the mainstream agencies. Synchronising the work of these organisations is a major logistical issue.

We have been working on this for 18 months, but it could take two more years before decentralisation is achieved. There is at least a year's work on things like providing a common information service and training people to understand all of the agencies, the sources of grants, the criteria for administering grants and so on. So the concept of the one-stop shop and the single point of contact is grand in theory, but it's very difficult to implement in practice.

The second thing we are trying to co-ordinate is the non-grant support services. There is a huge emphasis now on shifting from grants to non-grant support, with £100,000 to £120,000 available to agencies for soft support money. Again there is huge need for rationalisation to avoid duplication on resources.

The third, and by far the most difficult area, is that of joint planning and implementation. That requires a strategic framework into which you can invite local development agencies and partnerships to contribute their action plans. The mainstream agencies must be involved as well to say what they will be spending over the coming years, what they will be spending it on, and how those resources can be accessed. Those are just three practical examples of the difficulty of co-ordinating the work at county strategy level.

I take issue with the notion that these meetings can be at a non-executive level. Strategic management of these initiatives requires executive leadership of very high calibre; managers who can manage the process between the agencies, who can go in and kick down doors and talk to people about the process of co-ordination and sharing of resources. Unless that kind of executive leadership is given, integration of area-based plans simply won't happen in practice.

Give Communities a Powerful Voice

Anna McGonigle

Anna McGonigle is a member of UNISON and has recently been nominated to the Omagh District Partnership by the Irish Congress of Trade Unions (ICTU).

I have just become an ICTU nominee to the Omagh District Partnership. I know my people, I know the issues and the problems, but partnerships are new and uncharted waters. The contributions in this book suggest that partnerships could become a powerful way to tackle the problems and issues we face. But it is important to get the ideas and practice right from the outset.

As trade unionists, many of us have suffered the frustration of representing members, with their daily problems, only to find that we are ignored. Our lack of power often means that our role is diminished to that of trying to hold on to the remaining shreds of dignity for our members. Fair treatment, justice, dignity and dialogue – things I fight for as a trade unionist – should be at the heart of any partnership worthy of the name.

As President Robinson says in her foreword, the question of partnership is about how power is exercised and on whose behalf. Those who currently hold power must be prepared to pass it on to us at local level. My own experience makes me cautious about whether this can become a reality. We will take a risk with them, and they have to take a risk on us. We are ready and willing to exercise power, and to use it responsibly in the interests of fairness and equality. We have, not only a vision of a society based on equality and sharing, but considerable experience of fighting for that vision in a practical way.

Making partnerships work in an effective way will require a very considerable change in the way government bodies and agencies do business. They will have to take their responsibilities (I especially include my own) for delivering much more seriously than they have in the past. In a real partnership of equals, everyone's responsibilities - as well as how they meet them - must come under scrutiny. The traditional ways of decision-making have failed to deliver - that failure, and the reasons for it, have to be recognised.

We have the ingredients necessary to produce partnerships that can be a real force for social and economic change. But for those partnerships to attain any credibility, they must be outcome-oriented. There must be a visible impact on those in greatest need. Partnerships must be prepared to act as agents of change, but they must also ultimately enable those who have been excluded from social and economic development in their own communities to become their own agents for change. Many of us believe that this is not only feasible, but crucial, if relationships here are to be reconstructed on the basis of democratic responsibility and accountability.

In order to harness partnerships as a real force for change we need clear and enforceable ground rules. We need codes of practice that give equality a central priority and ensure equality-proofing of all aspects of the initiative. There must be criteria for the operation of the partnerships which ensure the inclusion of groups from areas of greatest need - both inside the decision-making structures and as recipients of resources and in setting standards which judge whether the initiative has really made a difference. The structures must be reformulated to give the communities of greatest need not just a voice, but a powerful voice.

There has to be honesty and openness from government and a commitment to open up opportunities for all those groups who have been excluded in the past. This presupposes that those in power are prepared to recognise that such honesty has been absent in the past dealings with local communities. Discrimination remains a major component of most of the social and economic decisions in the north and this must be recognised. The European dimension is clearly important here. Europe is not just a facilitator of the initiative, it must be a guarantor that resources and structures are used to produce greater equality and democratic involvement with a particular focus on those who need it the most - in fact rather than just in theory.

A Trade Union Perspective

Brendan Hodgers

Brendan Hodgers is an officer of the Amalgamated Transport and General Workers' Union (ATGWU). He is Vice Chair of the Dundalk Employment Partnership, and Chair of the Dundalk Trades Council.

I come from a union with the policies and traditions of free collective bargaining. At a certain level, therefore, we do not accept the partnership concept. When I became a member of the Dundalk Partnership six years ago I had been a die-hard trade unionist for 27 years and nothing was going to change me! But I came to realise that, even after 27 years, I hadn't made much of a dent in employers' attitudes and I came to the view that I had better try a different approach.

Then, when I went to the Department of the Taoiseach to find out more about how the Partnership was supposed to work, it became clear that the senior civil servants didn't know either. It was refreshing to find civil servants who, for once in their lives, didn't know what we needed!

Our experience in Dundalk has been a good one, with tangible results in terms of job creation. For example, one participant in the community employment scheme was particularly interested in the environment and convinced the financial institutions to shred their secret files instead of incinerating them. The partnership found the money for a feasibility study and his project now employs 43 local people. He has opened depots in Dublin and Cork and now ships paper direct to a mill in Canada.

Of course, there have been some failures too, but the important thing is that we have some resources and we can identify the additionality in terms of job creation. We have been empowered to put resources into the ideas and projects that people have talked about for years without being listened to. The important thing is that anything that can be identified as work should be turned into meaningful employment. If you work for nothing you'll never be unemployed.

We had a lot of discussion and debate about what form the Dundalk Partnership should take and what its terms of reference and constitution would be. We tried to define who makes up the community and who should represent the community. Of course we had suspicions about one another, but we found accommodation.

A kind of creativity emerged as the partnership opened doors for us. For example, I found myself sitting with an employer who, with my trade union hat on, I had been fighting for three years. Yet here we were on the board and we had to reconcile our differences and trust one another.

Partnerships - Can Arranged Marriages Work?

Geraldine Stafford

Geraldine Stafford was recently appointed Economic Development Officer of Strabane District Council in Northern Ireland. She previously worked in private industry in England and Dublin and spent four years managing a CRISP scheme including a rural enterprise centre in Northern Ireland.

Although the concept of partnerships is a new direction in Northern Ireland, Strabane District Council has been operating in partnerships of one type or another for many years. An example is its involvement with North West Region Cross Border Group, Tyrone Economic Development Initiative, and Tyrone West.

North West Cross Border Group is a four-tier partnership between Donegal County Council, Limavady Borough Council, Derry City Council and Strabane District Council. Although the group has not worked entirely in harmony, it has stayed together nonetheless. It achieved funding under the INTERREG programme, and has made an application under INTERREG II. Areas of co-operation include co-ordinating a strategy for a waste management programme, a marketing strategy for inward investment and tourism development.

The council's involvement with the Tyrone Economic Development Initiative (TEDI) includes a partnership of four councils in Tyrone - Cookstown, Dungannon, Omagh and Strabane. TEDI involves the private sector and it is committed to a joint approach to marketing Tyrone as a county for inward investment and exporting.

Tyrone West is another partnership involving Strabane. This partnership between Strabane and Omagh District Councils and was facilitated by LEADER I funding and funding from Leckpatrick Dairies. The board also includes representatives of NIPSA, the Ulster Farmers' Union, statutory bodies and the community sector. It has been awarded £1 million under a LEADER II initiative on much the same partnership make-up as the LEADER I initiative.

The Western Sperrins area-based strategy has been targeted by the Department of Agriculture Rural Development Division and again this area covers both Strabane and Omagh District Councils. This strategy has been instrumental in bringing together 15 community groups for the benefit of the Western Sperrins area. The intention is to develop a strategy in conjunction with the public sector and statutory services such as the Northern Ireland Tourist Board and DoE planning.

An arranged marriage

The council is leading the formation of a district partnership board to distribute funds allocated under EU peace and reconciliation funding. The chief executive and economic development officers of the various councils are responsible for pulling the partnership together, but they will have very little say in the composition of the partnership board or how the partnerships will be administered. The council, the private sector and trade unions have all agreed their representation on the board with the voluntary and community sector and statutory sector now finalising their delegates.

This partnership is like an arranged marriage with all the wrong ingredients for an equitable and harmonious partnership. The bridal parties have not yet met and the guidelines and criteria set by Brussels are dictating the union. There remain a number of questions which have not been answered. Do the various interests know why they are there? Can they agree a common purpose or shared vision while maintaining their identity? What commitment will the individuals and the public or statutory sector have to the voluntary and community sector?

To be successful, partnership requires individuals to change, adapt and compromise. Will the business sector have the patience when councillors are politicking? Can the councillors leave aside politics and work for the good of the partnership? Will the community or voluntary sector use the partnership to attack the establishment and will the establishment allow the empowerment of the communities? I am not convinced that all these problems can be resolved or accommodated. Frustration can also set in, especially among the community and business sectors, because of the expected pace of progress. But partnerships need time.

Having raised these questions, I raise another in conclusion.

What have we got to lose? For the inhabitants of the Strabane area, there is the opportunity for a real material gain through the EU peace and reconciliation fund. Also, if we can make the partnerships work, we will have achieved a truly bottom-up approach. In short, maybe an arranged marriage can work.

GIDEON MENDEL/NETWORK

Section Six
Afterword

Learning to Disagree

Phil Flynn and Inez McCormack

In June 1996, Phil Flynn retired as General Secretary of IMPACT, the leading public sector trade union in the Republic of Ireland. He is now Chairperson of ICC, Ireland's state-owned bank which specialises in serving small and medium-sized businesses. Inez McCormack is the Northern Ireland Regional Secretary of UNISON, the leading public service union in Northern Ireland and Britain's largest union.

The papers in this book are based on contributions to a joint IMPACT-UNISON conference held in Newcastle Co. Down in February 1996. As the leading public sector unions in Ireland, north and south, we decided to host the conference as a contribution to the development of practical policies for peace, jobs and economic and social development in Northern Ireland and the border counties, particularly in the areas of greatest need. The conference brought together an unprecedented mix of speakers and participants from every sector of social and economic life on both sides of the border and across the community divide - offering a wide range of views which is reflected in this book. Together, we explored the relationship between public services and the emerging culture of partnership - and the very different experiences, opportunities and dangers which the term 'partnership' has come to mean in Ireland and Britain. In particular, we focused on the opportunities partnership could offer in underpinning the Irish peace process by integrating the goals of social inclusion, economic and social regeneration and democratic accountability. We started from the view that people in the divided communities of Ireland have more to unite them than to divide them - a view which was more than endorsed by the conference and the papers in this book.

It was an ambitious conference, politically, conceptually and in format. In a sense, the conference itself was a practical expression of partnership between practitioners of various sorts actively engaged on a daily basis in social and economic development projects. It had an added poignancy because it was held in the week following the Canary Wharf bombing which marked the end of the IRA cease-fire. Naturally, we asked ourselves whether we should go ahead with the conference - but we spent little time in deciding that we should. Because both UNISON and IMPACT took the view that peace is not simply a matter for governments, politicians or paramilitaries. Peace is a concern - and a responsibility - for all of us as individuals, communities, organisations and enterprises of every kind.

In the event, the conference which gave birth to this collection of papers saw some 140 people meet at a time of measured and qualified hope to discuss how effective and democratic development could best be achieved. We found a lot of common ground, particularly in a shared belief that the European peace initiative, and other efforts for economic and social development in Ireland, should be used to target disadvantage and exclusion. If they are truly to be a force for change, these initiatives must also bring changes in the way decisions about economic and social development are made. Almost without exception, the papers in this book agree that any durable peace requires not just the taking of responsibility - but the sharing of responsibility. In turn, that requires the sharing of power and control over decision-making.

The contributors to this book have listened to, and learned from, each other. Their papers emphasise the importance of relationship building. They show a recognition that, if economic and social progress is to be real and durable, it requires fundamental changes in the way we do business with each other across sectors, communities and borders. And they reveal a realistic appreciation that, for all the difficulties, this moment in history offers an opportunity to take the risks necessary to make those changes. There has been a passionate and profound debate about the relationships between social justice, equality and good governance which has a relevance in both parts of the island of Ireland, in Britain, and beyond.

A strong theme that permeates this book is that, although there are many useful models, there is no simple blueprint for a success-ful and effective partnership. Every partnership is unique, pre-senting unique challenges, unique problems and requiring unique structures. But, at the same time, there is no alternative to finding ways of working together if we are to reach accommodations based on trust, recognition and respect for difference, and the realisation of those common goals that exist. This demands new forms of think-ing and acting, and the development of new, more appropriate struc-tures.

That is a daunting task - but we are not beginning from a standing start. There is a vast range of commitment, experience and expertise in communities, businesses, trade unions and the statutory sector. There is already much experience of working in partnerships and of the practical opportunities for social and economic progress they can offer - as well as the problems they can present. The debate encapsulated in this collection of papers is by no means starry-eyed about partnership. But it is driven by a recognition that partnership need not require the compromise of principles or the diminution of vision. What it does require is a focusing of energy on tackling prob-lems by developing clear, achievable goals and developing and set-ting criteria and structures capable of bringing visible and durable change.

The first meeting of the Northern Ireland Partnership Board was held five days after our conference. Not surprisingly, therefore, the ideas that emerged from the conference were carried over to the dis-cussion at that key meeting. It is indicative of a welcome shift in thinking that the meeting produced a discussion on gender balance which went beyond procedural aspects and recognised that differ-ences had to be respected and that questions of power and balance had to be addressed. Such debates soon become sterile if discussion does not move onto practical questions about getting things done, and then quickly on to action. But these practical matters must be informed and influenced by a genuine commitment to equality.

Neither was there any disagreement at the first Northern Ire-land Partnership Board meeting that the priority should be to tack-le disadvantage or that resources should be directed to those most in need. There was a recognition that, as soon as criteria for funding were agreed and understood, money should be distributed quickly where it would bring the most tangible results. But there was also a clear and determined understanding that business interests, community representatives, trade unions and political groups must face the challenge of economic regeneration and social change together - and share responsibility for the outcome. Movement on the ground is essential but, equally, there needs to be a huge investment in good and effective governance.

The focus on areas of greatest need was central to the aims and intentions of the conference. Not merely to highlight the initiatives that are already underway within communities but to link them in a practical way to the discourse of government, business and trade unions and to indicate that the development of partnerships - based on joint ownership of economic and social development - can lead to new and productive ways of making such areas a central part of our society and economy, rather than a peripheral concern.

The partnership model can challenge the traditional roles of public services, statutory bodies and government. It can redefine their role from that of gatekeeper, determining how resources are allocated, to that of agents, permitting and encouraging new voices to come forward and responding to those voices. For this to become a reality, these agencies must be committed to working as equals, particularly with those who have been excluded from decision-making. Social inclusion does not just mean providing more training, skills and jobs to those who have been denied them - important though that is. It means bringing those on the periphery into the heart of the decision-making process. Equally, it presents the community sector with the challenges of responsibility and accountability.

So, the partnership model is more than just a delivery mechanism; it is a means of building new civic relationships and devolving decision-making outwards from the centres of power towards the powerless. That demands respect for diversity and the inclusion of many interests, and all communities (no matter what their political allegiance) in the determination of criteria, goals and outcomes. As such, partnership could be a powerful democratic dynamic.

IMPACT and UNISON hosted our conference in the belief that real justice and sustainable peace in Ireland required more that just an end to the bombs and bullets. Then as now, it is clear that the path to peace is not always an easy one to travel. It demands effort - and change - from all of us. All of us are required to play an ever more positive, and ever more energetic, role in finding an agreed and durable political accommodation. That requires the removal of the injustices that have fuelled inequality and conflict on both sides of the political divide. If we can work together in partnership for the social change and economic development necessary to underpin a lasting peace we will have made a crucial step forward. Not by ignoring our differences but by learning to deal with them. By learning to disagree, and then transcending our disagreements

Appendix
Empowerment
through
Partnership

UNISON/IMPACT Conference
15th - 16th February 1996

List Of Participants

Sheila Adams
Footprints Women's Group. Community representative on Lisburn District Partnership.

Dave Anderson
National Executive Member, UNISON

Roger Bannister
National Executive Member, UNISON

Rodney Bickerstaffe
General Secretary, UNISON

Maggie Bierne
Research and Policy Officer, Committee on the Administration of Justice

Raymond Blaney
National Executive Member, UNISON

May Blood
Shankill Regeneration Strategy. ICTU representative on Belfast District Partnership

Lynne Brandon
Brownlow Community Trust

Al Butler
National Secretary, IMPACT

Marion Byrne
Area Development Management

Noreen Byrne
Chair, National Women's Council of Ireland

Miriam Cashell
Vice President, IMPACT

Peter Cassells
General Secretary, Irish Congress of Trade Unions

Margaret Cathcart
North Down Women's Aid. Community representative on North Down and Ards District Partnership

Paul Cavanagh
North West Community Network

Shay Cody
Deputy General Secretary, IMPACT

James Corrigan
Research Fellow, Institute of European Studies, Queen's University, Belfast.

Sarah Craig
Research Officer, Combat Poverty Agency

Ann Craven
Greencastle Women's Group. Community representative on Newtownabbey District Partnership

Carol Cullen
Tar Anall

Phil Curley
Municipal Employees Division, IMPACT

Theresa Devlin
Rural Development Network

Cherry Dickson
Magherafelt Women's Group

Pamela Dooley
Northern Ireland Regional Administrator, UNISON

Rita Donaghy
National Executive Member, UNISON

Lorraine Douglas
UNISON, London Region

Ian Duggan
Vice President, IMPACT

Terry Enright
Black Mountain Environmental Group

Wendy Evans
Vice President, UNISON

Sir David Fell KCB
Head of Northern Ireland Civil Service

Brian Ferguson
ICTU representative on Lisburn District Partnership

Mary Ferris
National Executive Member, UNISON

Phil Flynn
General Secretary, IMPACT

Hugh Frazer
Director, Combat Poverty Agency

John Freeman
President, ICTU

Maureen Gaffney
Chairperson, National Economic and Social Forum

Danny Gillespie
UNISON, Scottish Region

Evelyn Gilroy
Falls Community Forum. Community representative on Belfast District Partnership

Bob Gourley
Chair, ICTU Northern Ireland Committee

Ann Graham
Ballybeen Women's Centre. ICTU representative on Castlereagh District Partnership

Mavash Graham
Multi-cultural Resource Centre

Aubrey Halley
Honorary Secretary, IMPACT

Bernard Harbor
Information Officer, IMPACT

Elaine Harvey
Galway Centre for the Unemployed

Seamus Heaney
Community Facilitator, Creggan Neighbourhood Partnership

Eileen Howell
Director, Falls Community Council. Community representative on Belfast District Partnership

Brendan Hodgers
Chair, Dundalk Trades Council

Pat Ingram
President, UNISON

Edwina Jones
President, IMPACT

Tony Judd
Vice President, IMPACT

Oonagh Kane
Northern Ireland Joint Regional Convenor, UNISON

Paddy Keating
National Secretary, IMPACT

Pauline Keegan
Department of the Environment

Roisin Keenan
Fermanagh Women's Network

Carol Kennedy
ICTU representative on Ballymena District Partnership

Danny Kirrane
Manager, Co. Sligo LEADER Partnership

Joe Law
Counteract

Bernie Lillis
Honorary Equality Officer, IMPACT

Mary Lundy
State Enterprise Division, IMPACT

Liam Maskey
Intercom - North Belfast Community representative on Belfast District Partnership

Liz May
NIPSA

Peter Morris
National Research and Policy Director, UNISON

Marie Mulholland
Women's Support Network. ICTU representative on Co-operation North Advisory Committee

Irene Murphy
Shankill Women's Forum

Kenny McAdams
Disability Action

Geraldine McAteer
Manager, Upper Springfield Trust

Brendan McCarthy
Northern Ireland Joint Regional Convenor, UNISON

Dermot McCarthy
Department of An Taoiseach

Inez McCormack
Northern Ireland Regional Secretary, UNISON

Ann McCrystal
Magherafelt Women's Group. Community representative on Magherafelt District Partnership

Jim McCusker
General Secretary, NIPSA

Tony MCCusker
Director, Making Belfast work

John McFadden
Vice President, UNISON

Conal McFeeley
Northern Ireland Co-operative Development Agency. Community representative on Derry District Partnership

Eilin McGinley
MFG

Paddy McGinn
Area Development Management

Anna McGonigle
UNISON National Executive Member. ICTU representative on Omagh District Partnership

Anne McGovern
Research Department, UNISON

Patricia McKeown
Northern Ireland Deputy Regional Secretary, UNISON

Barrie McLatchie
Belfast Centre for the Unemployed

Michael McLoone
County Manager, Donegal County Council

Peter McLoone
General Secretary Designate, IMPACT

Eithne McLoughlan
Manager, MFG

Jean McMinn
ICTU representative on Craigavon District Partnership

Ann McVicker
Shankill Women's Centre. ICTU representative on Belfast District Partnership

Kevin Nelson
UNISON, North West Region

Martin O'Brien
Director, Committee on the Administration of Justice

Quintin Oliver
Director, Northern Ireland Council for Voluntary Action

Monina O'Prey
Northlands Centre

Dr. Mo O'Toole
Lecturer, University of Newcastle-upon-Tyne

Laurence Pollock
UNISON Journal

Sir George Quigley
Chair, Ulster Bank Ltd

Sean Redmond
National Secretary, IMPACT

Paul Roberts
Ashton Centre Development Ltd.

Rob Robertson
National Development Officer,
UNISON

Ken Rooney
Fountain Area Partnership

Ann Scallon
ICTU representative on Fermanagh
District Partnership

Colin Shillington
Business in the Community

Nicola Skinner
East Belfast Development Agency

Martin Snoddon
EPIC

Geraldine Stafford
Economic Development Officer,
Strabane District Council

Paul Sweeney
Department of the Environment

Marjorie Trimble
ICTU representative on Newtown-
abbey District Partnership

Noirin UiChleirigh
Chairperson, Glor na nGael

Dave Wall
Honorary Treasurer, IMPACT

Padraic A White
Chair, Northside Partnership
(Dublin)

Colin Wolfe
European Commission

Tracy Wright
Windsor Women's Centre

Patrick Yu
Northern Ireland Council for the
Ethnic Minorities